Death
and
Life

Otto Kaiser
and
Eduard Lohse

translated by John E. Steely

ABINGDON

Nashville

TOD UND LEBEN

DEATH AND LIFE

Library of Congress Cataloging in Publication Data

KAISER, OTTO, 1924-
   Death and life.
   (Biblical encounter series)
   Translation of Tod und Leben.
   Includes bibliographical references and index.
   1.   Death—Biblical teaching.   2.   Future life—
Biblical teaching.   3.   Resurrection—Biblical teach-
ing.   4.   Christian life—Biblical teaching.   I.
   Lohse, Eduard, 1924-   joint author.   II.   Title.
   III.   Series.
BS680.L5K313   236   80-21265

ISBN 0-687-10332-0

MANUFACTURED BY THE PARTHENON PRESS AT
NASHVILLE, TENNESSEE, UNITED STATES OF AMERICA

Contents

Translator's Preface

The work of translating this book has afforded me the opportunity of learning from its distinguished authors. Their mastery of their fields and their sensitivity to the issues involved will be manifest to the reader. It is my hope that others will share my experience of coming to grips with these issues and of discovering resources for instruction and comfort.

The staff of the Library of Southeastern Baptist Theological Seminary provided cheerful and capable assistance in finding English translations of quoted materials and in locating the corresponding English references to items cited in the notes. I thank them for their unfailing courtesy and help. A special word of gratitude is due also to my friends Sally and Ben Fisher for their encouragement and support. My warmest word of thanks must go to my wife, Donnie, who continues to be interpreter, teacher, and full participant in this undertaking.

John E. Steely

Wake Forest, North Carolina
January, 1980

Death and Life

"Today Ursel, our six-year-old"—thus Max Frisch relates in his journal—"suddenly interrupted her play and asked whether I would like to die. 'Everyone must die,' I said from behind my newspaper, 'but no one wants to die.' She thought a minute. 'I would like to die!' 'Now?' I asked, 'Really?' 'Not now, no, not now.' I lowered my newspaper to look at her; she was sitting at the table, mixing watercolors. 'But later,' she said, and started painting with quiet pleasure, 'later I would like to die.' "*

Who would answer the question whether he would like to die by saying that he is ready for it now? Death is the last enemy, says the apostle Paul (1 Cor. 15:26). But he adds that this enemy is disarmed, conquered, through the resurrection of Jesus Christ from the dead. For this reason he can declare that he has a desire to depart from the world and to be with Christ (Phil. 1:23). But this means nothing less than that he is ready to die gladly. However, he is no less ready to continue to serve the commission that has been given to him (*ibid*). How does it come about that death and life are regarded thus? What are the presuppositions? How did the people of the Old Testament deal with the question of the riddle of death and the meaning of life? In what fashion did they struggle with the problem of the justice of God and not abandon hope in the face of death? What was the ground of the expectation of the resurrection of the dead? And what considerations determined the understanding of death and life that the first Christians gained through the vision of their faith? Careful interrogation of the biblical writings should provide an answer and show that their utterances are involved in a discussion with basic questions of human life that confront people who think and act responsibly, now as then.

*M. Frisch, *Tagebuch 1946–1949*, pp. 349-50.

A.
DEATH AND LIFE IN THE OLD TESTAMENT

Death, resurrection, and immortality in the Old Testament and in early Judaism—considered in a religio-historical context

for C. Dieter Hinnenberg

I. The hope of immortality in the Wisdom of Solomon and the possibilities of a meditation on its history

**But the souls of the righteous
are in the hand of God,
and no torment will ever touch them.
(Wisdom of Solomon 3:1 RSV)**

In a grave crisis of the Jewish community in Alexandria in the middle of the first century B.C., a teacher whose name is unknown to us pled for the purity of Jewish faith and life by promising eternal life to the righteous and torment to the godless. His intellectual and spiritual legacy is handed down to us in the Greek Bible as the Wisdom of Solomon, and in Protestant translations is placed among the Apocrypha.[1] In a poem that is masterful in poetic power he portrays the inward attitude of people who, along with their religious commitment, have abandoned every ethical obligation and who acknowledge no other maxim for their conduct than to use all the means at their disposal to gain for themselves the greatest possible enjoyment of life. Thus they have no regard for the weaker members of society, the poor, widows, and the aged.

> Let our might be our law of right,
> for what is weak proves itself to be useless.
>   2:11 (RSV)

It is self-evident that the devout persons who faithfully held to the law of the fathers, by their very existence, had to appear to them as a challenge and to give occasion for persecutions, because they confronted them, as it were, as their bad conscience personified (cf 2:12 ff). The confession of these apostate Jews is in the last analysis a moving lamentation over the transiency and vanity of human life.

> Short and sorrowful is our life,
> and there is no remedy when a man comes to his end,
> and no one has been known to return from Hades.
> Because we were born by mere chance,
> and hereafter we shall be as though we had never been;
> because the breath in our nostrils is smoke,
> and reason is a spark kindled by the beating of our hearts.
> When it is extinguished, the body will turn to ashes,
> and the spirit will dissolve like empty air.
> Our name will be forgotten in time,
> and no one will remember our works;
> our life will pass away like the traces of a cloud,
> and be scattered like mist
> that is chased by the rays of the sun
> and overcome by its heat.
> For our allotted time is the passing of a shadow,
> and there is no return from our death,
> because it is sealed up and no one turns back.
>
> 2:1-5 (RSV)

In the view of the writer, they have come to these nihilistic conclusions only because, blinded by their own wickedness, they have not discerned God's secret purposes (2:21-22). According to his conviction, the truth about man is entirely different. Indeed, it only appears as though God has withdrawn and is not concerned about men, who thereby are left to their own devices and preferences, as though there were neither reward nor punishment. Thanks to its inclusion in Johannes Brahms' "German Requiem," we recognize at least the beginning of his refutation of this view as an old familiar text.

> The souls of the righteous are in the hand of God,
> and no torment will ever touch them.
> In the eyes of the foolish they seem to have died,

and their departure was thought to be an affliction,
and their going from us to be their destruction,
but they are at peace.
For though in the sight of men they were punished,
their hope is full of immortality.

3:1-4 (RSV)

The writer bases this hope on an interpretation in which he boldly draws his conclusion from biblical passages. On the very first page of the Mosaic Law (Gen. 1:26-27) it is stated that God created man in his own image. If God himself is the imperishable one (Ps. 90:2), then it follows that man, who is made in the image of God, himself must actually be destined for imperishability, and death has come into the world as a disruption of the original will of the Creator, through the cunning and the jealousy of Satan, without man's being thereby forever deprived of hope (cf Wisd. Sol. 1:13 ff with 2:21 ff). That the fall of the primal human pair could not have been caused by a mere serpent had to be obvious, in view of its momentous significance. There must have been a higher being involved in it, a fallen angel, who envied man for his being made in God's image and who for this very reason was expelled from the fellowship of the angels and now makes use of the serpent in order to get revenge; thus it is related to us in still another pre-Christian Jewish writing, the "Life of Adam and Eve."[2] The rest of the building blocks of the author's belief and thought can be discerned with a probability bordering on certainty. The basic question that troubled his community evidently consisted of the problem of what could be held to and maintained of God's promises of blessing to the obedient and his threats of cursing to the disobedient, when it was impossible to verify any connection between obedience and long life on the one hand and apostasy and an early death on the other hand. This question necessarily and persistently concerned Judaism in the centuries following the Babylonian captivity. And we shall see how in the Job-poem, the book of Ecclesiastes, and the proverbial wisdom of Jesus ben Sirach, people have attempted to give answers altogether different from those preferred here by the Alexandrian teacher.[3] If the Law was given by God, as the Scripture testified and as this conviction formed the foundation of the world-wide Jewish community of faith, then as long as the belief in the revelation of God's will in the Law and the belief in Israel's election above all other nations by this same God, the Creator of heaven and earth, remained unshaken, the solution to the premature death of the righteous person who was faithful to the Law and the long and better life of one who despised the Law could only be sought in a decision about the lot of both after death. And when the Jewish community, the Israel of God, in a world that was committed to serving idols, became a football for the great powers, then the people might hope, along with the Psalms and the prophetic books, that God would one day, in his own day, prove himself to be the Lord in the glorification of Israel in the sight of all the nations, and thereby put these others to confusion and put an end to the course of their contradictory history. For thus indeed one read it in the book of the prophet Isaiah:

> For thus says the Lord,
> who created the heavens
>   (he is God!),
> who formed the earth and made it
>   (he established it;
> he did not create it a chaos,
>   he formed it to be inhabited!):
> "I am the Lord, and there is no other.
> I did not speak in secret,
>   in a land of darkness;
> I did not say to the offspring of Jacob,
>   Seek me in chaos.
> I the Lord speak the truth,
>   I declare what is right.
>
> "Assemble yourselves and come,
>   draw near together,
>   you survivors of the nations! . . .
>
> "Turn to me and be saved,
>   all the ends of the earth!
> For I am God, and there is no other.

By myself I have sworn,
    from my mouth has gone forth in righteousness
    a word that shall not return:
'To me every knee shall bow,
    every tongue shall swear.'
"Only in the Lord, it shall be said of me,
    are righteousness and strength;
to him shall come and be ashamed,
    all who were incensed against him.
In the Lord all the offspring of Israel
    shall triumph and glory."

45:18-25 (RSV)

Thus the glorification of God in the sight of the nations and the demonstration of God's righteousness would occur together. And thus one might expect his judgment upon the nations, his glorification upon Zion and in all his people, and his judgment upon the dead to occur at the same time. And until that day, the souls of the righteous remain in God's hand and protection, at rest! Thus the afflictions suffered by his pupils and his community were capable of being solved.

But the righteous man, though he die early, will be at rest,
For old age is not honored for length of time,
nor measured by number of years;
but understanding is gray hair for men,
and a blameless life is ripe old age.

Wisd. Sol. 4:7-9 (RSV)

Moses, when he repeated the Law in the land of Moab, had solemnly declared to the fathers: "I call heaven and earth to witness against you this day, that I have set before you life and death, blessing and curse; therefore choose life, that you and your descendants may live, loving the Lord your God, obeying his voice, and cleaving to him; for that means life to you and length of days" (Deut. 30:19-20 RSV). If there is a life and a judgment after death, then these words were unshaken and unshakable in their validity. When the apostates appear, filled with fear at the reckoning-up of their sins and in terror at the evaluation of the righteous who have died prematurely, recognize their error and the futility of all their life and labors (cf. Wisd. Sol. 4:20—5:14), all the promises are fulfilled to the righteous.

> But the righteous live for ever,
> and their reward is with the Lord;
> the Most High takes care of them.
>
> Wisd. Sol. 5:15

A life that is under protection, an intermediate state in profound slumber, sheltered by God, and a new, eternal life—anyone who accepted this interpretation of the mystery of human existence, and in particular of the believer's existence, was relieved of the distresses that arose or could arise out of the tension between promises of Scripture and the everyday realities of a Jewish existence in an apparently overpowering pagan world, though the tensions could arise elsewhere as well. In spite of various independent ideas and an incontestable power of poetic construction, the solution of the problem of theodicy, the solution of the painful question as it is posed concerning the righteousness of God when even his own people are not spared suffering or an untimely death, probably was not altogether the work of the Alexandrian teacher. He had his predecessors, and presumably also some models for his writing.[4] Instead, his achievement rather lies in the fact that in spite of the hellenistic vocabulary that was unavoidable in his and his community's situation, and in spite of his language that was schooled in Greek philosophy and poetry, in the last analysis he provided a biblical foundation for this solution.[5] Hence his little writing, in contrast to various others that are thematically similar, was rightly preferred by the early church and was inserted into the church's own canon. It exhibits a reserve with respect to conceptions of the state of things after death and the ultimate awakening to eternal life. It also shows a paraenetic intention, admonishing the lukewarm and comforting those in tribulation. Because of these qualities, it demonstrates more clearly than do the comparable Jewish writings that the Jewish hope of the resurrection is not the result of mere wishful thinking or a speculation that is detached from actual existence, but is the answer to a question that is posed for man by the very mystery of his existence.

Man recognizes himself, as a thinking being and one who is aware of his own death, in a peculiar position in this world; this fact compels him to ask what is actually demanded of him as the being who is aware of his death. The fact that man senses his obligation to do the good for its own sake, that he is called upon sometimes to sacrifice his life for the sake of the truth itself and the truth and dignity of his neighbor without gaining any advantage therefrom except harmony with himself, points him to a reason and a grounding that itself robs death of its powers. In this sense, from anyone who accepts his death in dignity there issues a shock to his surrounding world that compels it to stand up to the question of its own death. If in the acceptance of his death man experiences the inescapable character of the claim of his mysterious ground of existence as peace and hope it is evident at the same time that, thanks to its source, this can be only a pure hope, one that transcends all efforts definitively to capture it in conceptual forms.[6] Also connected with this its source is the fact that the question of the immortality of the soul never can have an entirely satisfactory and ultimate theoretical solution. When the matter is weighed in calm reflection, in the end it is always possible to raise objections to the hope of immortality, its conceptual formulations, and its proofs, as Cebes immediately offers to his teacher Socrates in the *Phaedo:*

> Socrates, I agree to the other things you say, but in regard to the soul men are very prone to disbelief. They fear that when the soul leaves the body it no longer exists anywhere, and that on the day when the man dies it is destroyed and perishes, and when it leaves the body and departs from it, straightway it flies away and is no longer anywhere, scattering like a breath or smoke.[7]

Plato then has his revered teacher turn to his famous proof that all human learning is in fact an act of remembering; thus is provided the basis of the old saying that the souls "go there from here and come back here again and are born from the dead."[8] Toward the end of the dialogue, which concludes with the account of the death of Socrates and which as a whole covers the last day of the sage's life, Plato has his Socrates relate a myth of the fate of the soul after death. This is intended as a stimulus toward attaining moral perfection and discernment in this life. "For the prize is fair and the hope great."[9] And the reader will not forget that the one speaking here is a man who has been unjustly condemned to death, and his death is imminent, the same man who elsewhere taught his pupils that it is worse to commit an injustice than to suffer one.[10]

As is well known, Plato offered still another proof for the immortality of the soul, one that has enjoyed greater influence upon the belief and thought of later generations than that of learning as a remembering, which is indissolubly bound up with his doctrine of ideas. According to this proof, anything that moves under its own power is without beginning and is imperishable. Since the body that is inhabited by a soul moves under its own power, in contrast to a body that does not have a soul, that moves only under external impulses, the soul, as that which moves itself, is therefore immortal.[11] It has been said that these proofs, like the proofs of the existence of God, necessarily already presuppose what they propose to prove. Thus in the last analysis they only attempt to accentuate the awareness of what man actually has always known as a mystery of his existence and the ground of his existence.[12] Thus anyone who is going to be persuaded by them must already have experienced the presence of God and his own eternity in the assumption of his finitude or in an ethical life-and-death decision that he has made solely for its own sake.[13] For other people, they are an indicator pointing to a reality that is available for disclosure to them if they will let themselves be set free from the self-forgetfulness of an existence that takes refuge in illusions, so that in the acceptance of authentic being of their existence that has fallen victim to death, at the same time they gain the assurance of their eternal security.

In the following pages we will trace out the course of history of beliefs about death in the Old Testament and Judaism. This is prompted primarily by the fact that we are children of a historically schooled age who are conscious of the differences in the self-interpretation of human existence that have appeared in the course of history. But we have also become aware, in reading the Bible, of the fact that the Old Testament utterances about death may be read in two different senses that, at least to a considerable extent, are in direct opposition to each other. On the one hand, there is the sense of the Alexandrian teacher of the Wisdom of Solomon, whom we heard at the outset. On the other hand, there is the sense of the New Testament interpretation, a christological interpretation that exerts an influence upon the formation of the later ecclesiastical tradition and that finds even the mystery of the resurrection of Jesus Christ in the Old Testament texts. Like the biblical faith itself as a whole, so also the hope that belongs to that faith has a history which contemporary faith may subsequently invoke. Anyone who concerns himself with this history must consider the question whether there is dominant in the history a perspective according to which faith has been led, in the course of history, to a deepened understanding of itself or, on the contrary, has fallen victim to illusion. In the course of this study we shall take note of some rituals and perspectives of faith from other religions and cultures. With our present level of knowledge, we can hardly give assured answers to questions about specific connections and lines of dependence among these various religions and cultures. Nevertheless, what emerges in the study may offer the occasion for considering whether there was a *consensus gentium*, an agreement of the various peoples, in the belief of the ancients concerning a life after death, as they at least thought they discerned it in the anxiety, common to all humanity, that is aroused by the question of what will happen after death.[14]

II. Death as Destiny

**Lord, let me know my end,
and what is the measure of my days;
let me know how fleeting my life is!
(Psalm 39:4 RSV)**

In Wisdom of Solomon 2:23 the Alexandrian teacher sets forth the thesis that man's destiny of incorruption, which corresponds to God's eternity, is contained in his being made in God's image. For historical retrospect, this suggests to us the further question whether in the view of the biblical creation story of Genesis 1:1 ff or of the story of Paradise and the fall in Genesis 2:4 ff, man was created mortal or immortal. The creation story, which now serves to introduce the entire Bible, understands man's being in the image of God, notwithstanding the realism that at least primarily marks the account, as man's being destined to serve as God's representative on this earth; this much may now be regarded as undisputed. This destiny has its specific expression in the text in the commission to have dominion over the beasts (Gen. 1:26-27).[15] The question of his mortality is not explicitly considered in that context. However, the genealogy of the patriarchs before the Flood (Gen. 5), which belongs to the same Priestly stratum of the document, gives no indication that men were originally created immortal. It is assumed, however, that the men of the historical period after the Flood live to an age that is only a fraction of the 930 years granted to Adam or the 969 years granted to Methuselah. Hence one may say that the Priestly writer assumed the normal lifespan actually intended for man is a thousand years.[16]

The matter becomes more problematical when we turn to the story of Paradise and the fall that follows the creation story. The man and the woman, by eating the fruit of the forbidden tree of the knowledge of good and evil, incurred the penalty of death (cf Gen. 2:16-17). Then God put a curse upon the serpent for having incited them to this disobedience (3:14-15), in order then to pronounce his words of destiny concerning the future lot of women and men (3:16-19). In this connection the word concerning the man's destiny concludes with the well-known "till you return to the ground, for out of it you were taken; you are dust, and to dust you shall return" (RSV).[17] Man's having been formed from the dust, the loose soil of the earth, had already been related in 2:7 in anticipation of this outcome. The question that must now be addressed to the saying about man's destiny is whether it has to do with the disclosure of the mortality that belongs to man's essential nature or is a determination of his fate of death that only now for the first time is set. In favor of the latter interpretation, one could be tempted to argue from the word of destiny concerning woman and the curse upon the serpent. In both cases, there is decreed for the one addressed a new mode of existence that reaches deep into

the physical realm. But again, and in this context by no means
the last time, one must recall the commandment concerning
the garden in 2:16-17: it declares that the death penalty will be
the punishment for disobedience.[18] Thus there can be no
suggestion that in the opinion of the narrator man had been
created immortal and had lost the corresponding attribute
through the fall. And yet one can say that the view of death was,
for man who was still in his innocence and ignorance, hidden
and concealed, as it were, by the presence of God.[19] Or, to put it
another way: death acquired its terror through sin.

If nothing were said explicitly in the narrative in Genesis
2:9 and 3:22 about the tree of life, probably no one would have
the idea of relating the problem of immortality to it. The notes
about the tree of life, in any editorial context whatsoever, have
only subsequently been connected with the story of the tree of
knowledge. This is placed beyond any doubt by the present
narrative context: in 3:3 the woman speaks to the serpent in
quite neutral terms of the forbidden tree as the tree in the
middle of the garden. In fact, the point of the entire dialogue
consists precisely in the fact that the serpent discloses to the
woman the secret of the tree. She has no inkling that it is the
tree of knowledge. And we must assume that her husband is in
the same state of ignorance. However, the commandment
concerning the garden in 2:16-17 already has spoken of the tree
of knowledge. And moreover, nothing at all is said there about
its being the tree in the middle of the garden. The logic of the
context of the narrative would make it necessary to identify the
tree in 2:17 as it is in 3:3, as the tree in the middle of the garden.
If we look from this perspective at the verse in which the two
trees are first mentioned (2:9) we are struck with the impression
that the mention of the tree of knowledge is very awkward.
Nevertheless, the reading here again may originally have
spoken only of the "tree of the knowledge of good and evil" that
was planted "in the midst of the garden." We can clarify the
matter still further if we only note that 3:22 and the major part of
3:24 belong to the "tree of life" stratum of the material.[20] Of
course, this all the more raises the question as to what intention
was operative in the combining of the tree-of-life motif with the
story of the fall. We read in 3:22: "Then the Lord God said,

'Behold, the man has become like one of us, knowing good and evil; and now, lest he put forth his hand and take of the tree of life, and eat, and live for ever. . . . ' " We need only to look at this verse to realize that for this narrator, too, man was by no means created immortal. If man were immortal—thus runs the conviction that stands in the background—he would have no need of God; he would actually be equal to God. It is necessary to keep in mind the point in the entire narrative at which the motif of the tree of life comes into play: it is only in view of fallen man that it plays a role in the story. Or, to put it in another way, making use of the mythical symbols: immortality first comes into the field of vision of fallen man, man who is separated from God. But he cannot cross the boundary of death that is set for him. He is mortal.[21]

The ancient motif of the envy of the gods echoes in Genesis 3:22. We encounter it in undisguised form in the Babylonian myth of Adapa. According to this myth, Adapa had been created and equipped with wisdom by Ea, the god of water and of wisdom. Adapa was summoned before the celestial god Anu because he had broken the wing of the south wind. Before he made his way to Anu, Ea counseled him not to touch any of the food that would be set before him in heaven, since it would be the bread and water of death. So Adapa refused the hospitality, with the bread and water of life, that had been offered to him by Anu's magnanimous command, and had to return to the earth mortal. [22] The behavior of the god Ea is not explained in the parts of the epic that are extant. But one certainly may draw the conclusion that the creator of man wanted to keep his creature from gaining immortality and thus becoming fully his equal. Thus the mythological formulation of envy of the gods is in the last analysis an expression of the twofold awareness that man as a rational being is akin to the gods and as a mortal being is separated from the gods, whose immortality, in analogy to the dependence of human life upon the regular taking of nourishment, is interpreted as a consequence of their partaking of a divine magical nourishment.[23]

The theme of the search for eternal life occupies a central place in the Babylonian *Gilgamesh Epic,* one of the greatest poetic compositions of world literature. It lets the reader be an observer of how the search for eternal glory by Gilgamesh, the young king of Uruk, is changed, in view of the death of his friend Enkidu, into the search for eternal life.[24] When his companion shrank from the excursion against the mighty Huwawa who dwelt in the cedar forest, Gilgamesh proudly declared that he would give his life, which was mortal anyway, for the sake of fame.

> Who, my friend, can ascend (as man) to heaven?
> Only the gods live forever with Shamash.[25]
> As for men, their days are numbered,
> Only Wind remains, whatever they do!
> But already here you live in fear of death—
> What has become of your heroic strength?
> I will go before you, and then you will only need
> To call to me, "Forward! Have no fear!"
> And if I die, I will make a name for myself.
> Then they will say, "Gilgamesh has fallen
> In battle with the terrible Huwawa." . . .
> For truly I will lift up my hand,
> Will cut down the cedar;
> I will make a name for myself that will endure.[26]

But then when Enkidu died, after suffering grievous fevers and dreams, after they had struck down Huwawa together and had even killed the bull of heaven, a panic seized the hero. He then set out on the way to Utnapishtim, his ancestor who had been taken away by the gods after the flood, in order to learn from him how he had gained admission into the circle of the gods and attained eternal life. Thus he discovered that there is an immense difference between a theoretical and a practical knowledge about man's finiteness. On the way to Utnapishtim he meets a barmaid, Siduri, on the shore of the sea. Beyond this sea lie the waters of death, and again beyond there, at the distant mouth of the stream, lies the eternal dwellingplace of his ancestor. Here on the shore of the sea he sings his song of lamentation to the barmaid.

My friend whom I loved with all my heart,
    He who went through all the dangers with me,

Enkidu, my friend whom I loved so,
  He who went through all the dangers with me—
The sad lot of humankind took him away.
I wept for him six days and seven nights,
I would not concede that he was being taken away to burial
Until the worms fastened upon his face.
In the fear of death, then, I wandered through the wilderness,
  the fate of my friend lay heavy on my heart.
Back and forth I wandered through the wilderness,
  the fate of Enkidu lay heavy upon me.
How can I fall silent, how can I be still?
My friend whom I loved so has turned to dust,
  Enkidu, my friend, has turned to dust!
And I—must I like him lie down
  never again to rise?
Now, O barmaid, since I have seen your face—
Let me not see the face of death, which I fear so much.[27]

The barmaid's answer is utterly realistic. It finds its substantive parallels all the way from the ancient Egyptian harpists' songs,[28] through the Old Testament's "Let us eat and drink, for tomorrow we die" (Isa. 22:13 RSV) and the kindred exhortations of Ecclesiastes to enjoy transient life,[29] and the Greek lyricists,[30] to the ever new variations that Horace gave to his *carpe diem*.[31]

Gilgamesh, where are you hurrying to? You will never find that life for which you are looking. When the gods created man they allotted to him death, but life they retained in their own keeping. As for you, Gilgamesh, fill your belly with good things; day and night, night and day, dance and be merry, feast and rejoice. Let your clothes be fresh, bathe yourself in water, cherish the little child that holds your hand, and make your wife happy in your embrace; for this too is the lot of man.[32]

In essence this admonition is to be attributed to the conviction of the poet. Gilgamesh, however, is not willing to bow to it; instead, he persists in making his voyage to Utnapishtim and inquires of him how at the end of the great flood the blessing of deification had been bestowed upon him and his wife Enlil[33] and they had been transported to the mouth of the distant streams, the Babylonian Elysium. After Utnapishtim had vividly demonstrated to his grandson his human limitation, by putting him to a test that he did not pass, of going without sleep for six days and seven nights, he commissioned the ferryman, Urshanabi, to accompany Gilgamesh homeward. When Enlil, full of compassion for her grandson, asked for a reward for his labors, Utnapishtim entrusted to him the secret of the magical plant that grows in the depth of the sea, the eating of which brings back one's youth. The hero was able in fact to secure the plant from the depths; but when he stopped along the way homeward to wash off the dust of travel in a pool, the serpent stole it. Even today one can observe the result, when the serpent renews its youth by shedding its skin! But there was nothing left for Gilgamesh but to return to his home city of Uruk. Yet he obviously has been changed; for, proud of his work, he shows Urshanabi the great walls of his city. He has come to understand that there is no profit in rebelling against the fate of death that is imposed upon man; therefore he can return to the task that life sets for him. The exception that the gods have made, the bestowal of eternal life upon Utnapishtim, cannot be obtained by force through human effort. And thus, as an exception, it only proves the rule that all men must die.

In the description of the dwelling place of Utnapishtim, we quite naturally made use of the name of the isles or realm of the blessed, Elysium, familiar to us from ancient literature; the comparison is entirely appropriate. We need only to note the report of the blond hero Menelaus, the ruler of the peoples, who has happily returned home from the Trojan adventures. In the *Odyssey* IV.561 ff, the son of Odysseus, who has been searching for his father after the father had failed to return home, is thus instructed by Menelaus about the prophecy that had been communicated to him by the water god Proteus concerning his own future fate.

As for your own end, Menelaus, you shall not die in Argos, but the gods will take you to the Elysian plain, which is at the ends of the world. There fair-haired Rhadamanthus reigns, and men lead an easier life than anywhere else in the world, for in Elysium there falls not rain, not hail, nor snow, but Oceanus breathes ever with a west wind that sings softly

from the sea and gives fresh life to all men. This will happen
to you because you have married Helen, and are Zeus'
son-in-law.[34]

Thus, just as Menelaus, because of his being the son-in-law of
the king of the gods, was to be transported to the distant land
which is elsewhere described as the blessed isles near the
vortex of the ocean,[35] other demigods of the Greek saga-tradi-
tion were also granted a similar destiny.[36] Thus here too, these
are the exceptions that prove the rule.[37]

It is another exception when in the book of Genesis the
priestly writer tells that Enoch, the great-grandfather of the
biblical hero of the Flood, Noah, after a life that was lived in
fellowship with God, was taken away by God. The narrator leaves
it with a simple, monosyllabic note, "And Enoch walked with
God, and was not; for God took him (*lāqach*)" (Gen. 5:24).[38] The
"Book of the Watchmen" from the third or early second century
B.C., which was later incorporated into a more comprehensive
Book of Enoch (Enoch 1–36), declares[39] that no man knows where
Enoch was concealed (Enoch 12:1). It is the Book of Jubilees,
composed toward the end of the second century B.C., that first
offers the information that Enoch had been transported into the
Garden of Eden, that is, into Paradise (cf Jub. 4:23 with Gen.
2:8).[40] As one who was to all intents and purposes God's confidant,
he was commended to later times as the recipient of secret
revelations concerning the celestial and earthly mysteries of the
cosmos, the calendar, the angels, and history.

The account of the transporting of the prophet Elijah,
according to 2 Kings 2:11-12, is no less laden with mystery. In
the presumably earliest version, handed down in verses 11a
and 12b, a fiery chariot, drawn by fiery horses, suddenly
appeared and separated Elijah from his companion and
successor, Elisha. Then Elijah disappeared, and Elisha tore
his robes as a sign of grief. A later editor, in keeping with the
sense of the basic text, has added in verse 11b that Elijah
ascended to heaven in a whirlwind (cf Ecclus. 48:9), and has
placed in the mouth of Elisha the lament that King Joash of
Israel is supposed to have uttered beside Elisha's own
deathbed, "My father, my father! the chariots of Israel and its

horsemen!" (2 Kings 13:14).[41] It is an obvious assumption that the earlier narrator gave his report in such a reserved fashion out of reverence toward the heavenly world of Yahweh. But it is an equally natural conjecture that in this strange conveyance we are dealing with nothing other than Yahweh's own battle chariot, his stormcloud-chariot drawn by the cherubim, the cloud-horses.[42] In answer to the question as to the destination of this journey, one will think of the heavenly (cloud) palace of Yahweh, a conception which Israel may well have borrowed, along with that of the cloud-chariot, from Canaanite mythology.[43] While it remains an open question as to what the Priestly author thought of as the destination of the patriarch who was taken away, here we meet the idea of one's being taken up into heaven. This motif is also familiar in Greek mythology. As is shown by the most common example of Ganymede, which at the same time exhibits an entirely different sense of life (cf Iliad XX.231 ff), there it is a matter primarily of the apotheosis of the handsome youth.[44]

The cases of raising people from the dead that are attributed to Elijah and Elisha are on an altogether different plane, since what is involved there is a temporary and not a final liberation from the power of death (cf 1 Kings 17:17 ff and 2 Kings 4:18 ff).[45] We must also mention the unique narrative of 2 Kings 13:20-21: When a band of Moabite marauders suddenly appeared on the scene while a man was being buried, his body was hastily thrown into Elisha's tomb. Then, by simply touching the bones of Elisha, the man was revived.[46] This miracle story, which was told to the greater fame of the prophet and the prophets, belongs in the context of our present inquiry alongside the two cases that we have just mentioned. Here too what was involved was a temporary and not an eternal deliverance from death.

Thus the fact remains, for Mesopotamian man as well as for the Greek and the Israelite man of antiquity and far beyond these limits, the exceptions only proved the rule, that the death of man is an unalterable destiny. "We must all die, we are like water spilt on the ground, which cannot be gathered up again" (2 Sam. 14:14), the wise woman from Tekoa instructs King David in order to exhort him to act while there is still time. If we may trust the testimony of the Ugaritic literature, this conviction was also shared by the Canaanites, the earlier inhabitants of the land and later neighbors of the Israelites. In the *Aqhat Epic,* which unfortunately is extant only in fragmentary form, there is an episode which exhibits an extraordinarily strong reserve toward all myths that tell of raptures. The goddess Anat, the violent consort of the storm-god Baal who dwells in his cloud-palace on the mountain Zafon, promises to give the prince Aqhat immortality (*blmt*) if he will give her the bow that has been made for him by the smith-god Khasis. But the prince answers her soberly (*Aqhat* II, VI, 33 ff):

> Lie not unto me, O virgin; is not thy lying unseemly to a hero? What does a man get as [his] ultimate fate? What does a man get as the ultimate lot? Glaze will be poured on [my] head and quicklime upon my pate; And I shall die the death of all [men] and myself indeed shall die.

But of course he had to pay for his refusal and even more for the subsequent rejection of the woman in the goddess.[47]

Amazing to us is the attitude with which the ancients as a rule contemplated their death. Lycaon, Priam's son, had saved himself from the floods of the swirling Scamander, only to fall into the hands of Achilles. In vain the youth begged for his life. But the son of Peleus, enraged by the death of his beloved Patroclus, knew no pity.

> Therefore, my friend, you too shall die. Why should you whine in this way? Patroclus fell, and he was a better man than you are. I too—see you not how I am great and goodly? I am son to a noble father and have a goddess for a mother, but the hands of doom and death overshadow me all as surely. The day will come, either at dawn or dark, or at the noontide, when one shall take my life also in battle, either with his spear, or with an arrow sped from his bow. (*Iliad* XXI, 106 ff)

Then the youth surrendered himself to his fate. When his knees failed him, he extended his arms wide to receive the fatal blow.[48]

In spite of the impression that is suggested to the contrary by Wisdom of Solomon 4:7 ff, there is a contrast between the view of premature and violent death held by the Greeks and that of the Israelites. Moreover, there is a contrast between these two that grows even sharper in the passage of time. Over against the famous verse of the comic poet Menander, handed down by Plutarch, "He whom the gods love dies young,"[49] we find in the Old Testament the plea, "O my God, take me not away in the midst of my days" (Ps. 102:24).[50]

As an example of a calm and considered perspective on one's own death we may invoke the case of the Gileadite Barzillai. This octagenarian notable had cared for King David in Mahanaim during the ruler's forced exile at the time of Absalom's rebellion. When the danger was over and the king returned to Jerusalem, Barzillai escorted him in honor to the crossing of the Jordan. In gratitude for his kindness, David wanted to take him to the royal court, but the old man refused. Too old to enjoy the advantages of the life at court, he proposed his son for the honor in his place. "Let your servant return," he asked, "so that I may die in my own city, near the grave of my father and my mother" (2 Sam. 19:38).

III. The future
of those who have died

**There is neither work nor thought,
neither knowledge nor understanding,
in Sheol, to which you are going.
(Eccles. 9:10)**

Such a gloomy outlook on death as we have seen in the preceding chapter, and as we also know it from our own immediate experience, obviously is connected with the primal fear which itself, in turn, is related in man's mind to this incapacity of his, among all his possibilities, the only one that is both certain and absolute. Everything that a man hopes for, plans, undertakes, or fears in his life can turn out differently.[51] Only this one thing will certainly come to him: his death. Living, he knows no other existence but his present bodily and earthly existence. He can anticipate all possible experiences but that of his own death. Alien death, however, signifies for him the end of any possibility of communication with the deceased, and the lifeless body of the deceased one cannot be held back from decay. Therefore for every man death holds sway as a basic, primal fear. It appears to degrade him—a being who thinks, feels, and wills, and who perceives himself as a subject himself and an end in himself—into an object and to annihilate him, in spite of his peculiar, distinctive dignity, which is his alone and characterizes him alone among all the others in this world. He experiences it in beholding the corpse of a person whom he has loved or respected. At the same time, it arouses in him, along with the primal fear that is present at least beneath the surface and that exhausts him, a primal pain. With every separation and bereavement, the already sure prospect of his own death looms over him with even more certainty. The solidarity of all men, which is based upon their sharing the same nature, as those who are intended to possess the same worth and dignity, persists in the fact that, if he is not blinded by hatred or scorn, the view of the body even of an unknown person or an enemy moves him, so that he grants to the body the honor of lamentation and burial, and thus does not regard it as a mere object.[52]

But precisely his being different compels man to pose the question of his own and his companions' future. In the attempt to take away the terror from it, man can, on a level of consciousness characterized by a detached reflection about himself and this world, attempt to give himself an answer like that which the Platonic Socrates, in his defense speech, clothed in the general assertion, "To fear death, O men, is nothing other than to think that man would be wise to be without it."[53] For if man cannot anticipate the experience of his death and can have that experience only when he himself comes to his own death, he cannot know whether dying means for him an evil or a blessing. "For no one knows what death is, not even whether it is not for man the greatest among all goods."[54] And then for the second possibility he posed the famous alternative, which because of its simplicity and naturalness has never been forgotten by anyone who has heard of it: "The state of being dead is one or the other of two things: when a man is dead, he is the same as nothing, not having any kind of sensation of anything, or, as is also said, it is a removal and relocation of the soul from here to another place."[55]

To be sure, Socrates did not create his own calm assurance in the face of death out of such reflections, but rather out of what he described as the failure to appear of any warning through "the sign," "the daimonion," his divine companion.[56] In the moral decision to surrender his life solely because of the issues involved in the decision itself, which corresponds to the claim that is contained in the very fact of being human, he experiences his eternality as the certainty that for the man who stands firm in his commitment, there can be no evil either in life or in death. And thus even the masters of his destiny and his fate, the gods, cannot allow him to fall into death.[57]

Let us turn back to the Socratic alternative concerning the future of the deceased. The former of the two possibilities suggested as it were a deep, dreamless sleep. And if it is the farewells that burden the heart of a man as he faces his own death,[58] he will know no more of these. One might paraphrase this set of circumstances with the words of Koheleth, in the book of Ecclesiastes: "The dead know nothing, and they have no more reward; but the memory of them is lost. Their love and their hate and their envy have already perished, and they have no more forever any share in all that is done under the sun" (Eccles. (9:5b-6). And in this same mood many in antiquity gave expression to their conviction in their epitaph: "I never was, I am no more. I know nothing about it; it has nothing to do with me."[59] This confession can be summed up in six initial letters: "n. f. n. s. n. c.," standing for the Latin "Non fui, non sum, non curo," that is, "I have not been, I am not, I do not trouble myself about it."[60] And like the Preacher in Ecclesiastes, who connects with the conclusion as to the utter nothingness of the deceased the admonition, "Go, eat your bread with enjoyment, and drink your wine with a merry heart" (Eccles. 9:7 RSV), the epitaph allows a similar exhortation to be addressed to the reader: "And you who live, eat, drink, play, come!"[61]

Of course it cannot be all that simple a matter to achieve calm in the prospect of utter forgetfulness of the deceased, when the Preacher precedes this assertion with another, making use of a proverb: "A living dog is better than a dead lion. For the living know that they will die, but the dead know nothing" (Eccles. 9:4b-5b). Because of its constant presence as the only assured possibility, death gives rise to a continuing uneasiness for life. But on the other hand, life itself is the disturbance of death. And both must be seen if there is to be a sufficient answer to the questions posed by death.

The texts that have been considered thus far create a false impression in view of the total historical reality, insofar as they suggest that only this Socratic alternative is open to man in his death, either to sink into eternal, unconscious sleep, in a nothingness that is devoid of all sense, or, knowing and perceiving, to arrive at another place and to enter into the new fellowship of the dead. The second alternative then is in fact also discussed explicitly in this explication.[62] But for the Greeks as well as for the people of the ancient Orient, including the Israelites, there was at first no such alternative. The two prospects, the communion of the departed in another place and the deep unconsciousness of the deceased, rather coincided for them, in the shadowy existence of the underworld.

But did the Old Testament know at all of such a shadowy realm as is familiar to us from Greek and Latin poetry and philosophy, or was it not rather "all over" for the Israelite when death came? It certainly was "all over" insofar as the dead, who were in the realm designated by the word "Sheol,"[63] an enigmatic word that perhaps actually signifies only "under-world," were definitively cut off from life on this earth. And it was "all over" also in the sense that the deceased in that realm sank into utter unconsciousness. In this twofold sense the poet of the book of Job can let his sufferer lament the lot of humanity.

> Man that is born of woman is of few days, and full of
> trouble.

He comes forth like a flower, and withers;
he flees like a shadow, and continues not. . . .

For there is hope for a tree,
    if it be cut down, that it will sprout again,
    and that its roots will not cease.
Though its root grow old in the earth,
    and its stump die in the ground,
yet at the scent of water it will bud
    and put forth branches like a young plant.
But man dies, and is laid low;
    man breathes his last, and where is he?
As waters fail from a lake,
    and a river wastes away and dries up,
so man lies down and rises not again;[64] . . .

. . . the waters wear away the stones;
    the torrents wash away the soil of the earth;
    so thou destroyest the hope of man.[65]
Thou prevailest for ever against him, and he passes;
    thou changest his countenance, and sendest him away.
His sons come to honor, and he does not know it;
    they are brought low, and he perceives it not.
He feels only the pain of his own body,
    and he mourns only for himself."
                     (14:1-2, 7-12*a*, 19-22 RSV)[66]

Going beyond this, it would be mistaken to conclude from this characterization of man's lot of death and his entering into "the land of forgetfulness" (Ps. 88:12) that according to the Israelite belief man was utterly annihilated upon his death. So, just as people regarded endangered life as having already fallen victim to the power of death and the underworld, on the other hand death was seen as the weakest form of life.[67] What survived down there below therefore was not simply nothing, but a shadowy, ghostly double of the living, his "soul," or, as we must put it more precisely in light of a soon-to-be-gained insight, his "death-soul" in the form that he had possessed at the moment of his departure.[68] Only under this presupposition can we explain the belief that in the case of a special fate that affects their descendants, the presence of the deceased can be discerned in the vicinity of their burial places; this is illustrated

in the case of the matriarch Rachel, whose weeping, it was
believed, could be heard at her tomb in Ramah at the time of
the defeat of her sons, the inhabitants of the northern kingdom
(cf Jer. 31:15 with Gen. 35:16, 19).[69] And only under this
presupposition can we explain that King Saul in his desperate
situation, obstructed by his enemies and abandoned by God,
turned to the woman at Endor in order to make inquiry of the
departed Samuel concerning his fate (1 Sam. 28). When the
woman who conjured up the dead described to the king the
"god" who ascended out of the depths as an old, bearded man
wearing a mantle, Saul knew that the prophet Samuel had
come, and he threw himself to the ground. Saul wanted the
prophet, not some insignificant, uninformed soul. Obviously
even death itself as such does not bestow any supernatural
capacities. It is well known how in the nocturnal scene the ghost
addressed the king with his "Why have you disturbed me and
brought me up here?" then to predict an end for him and his
sons on the following day.

If we follow out the history of the Hebrew designations for
those who conjure up the dead to the extent necessary for our
train of thought, we soon encounter religio-historical parallels
which allow us to fill out the picture of the souls of the dead. The
"seers" and—here we must introduce the Hebrew word—
" *'oboth*", variously rendered in the translations of 1 Samuel
28:3 as "mediums," "those that had familiar spirits," and
"conjurors," are quite obviously mantic figures. In Isaiah 8:19
the two words recur, the "seers" and, over against them, the
" *'oboth*" as spirits of the deceased.[70] And from Isaiah 29:4 we
learn how these spirits made themselves heard: with a low,
birdlike, twittering voice they speak out of the earth.

We have already noted, in connection with Rachel's
haunting her tomb, the special connection of the spirits of the
departed with their burial places.[71] Because of this belief, it
appears that in conjuring up these spirits the preferred custom
was to gather at their tombs by night. The choice of the
nighttime arises out of the general popular belief that before the
dawn the spirits and demons had to return to their dark abode
(cf Isa. 65:4; 1 Sam. 28:8; and Gen. 32:27).[72] Turning again to
the history of the meaning of the word *'ob* (plural *'oboth*), we

note that the word, which first apparently denoted the spirit of the deceased and then the person who conjured up the dead, also could have a third, technical meaning, which with good reason will be regarded as the earliest; for it is more plausible that the name for a means employed should subsequently assume the meaning of that which is wrought thereby and then of the one employing the means, than it is to think of the history of the meaning as developing in the other direction. Thus the " 'ob" in 1 Samuel 28:8 is hardly a spirit of divination; for there is nothing in the story to indicate that the woman is performing in the role of a medium who is possessed, as is related in spiritualistic stories even in the present time.[73] According to evidence which can be adduced with great probability, the enigmatic word appears already to have come from the language of the pre-Semitic inhabitants of southern Mesopotamia, the Sumerians, and made its way as a loan-word into the Accadian, the language of the Babylonians and Assyrians, and then spread into Asia Minor. Its basic meaning then would be "hole" or "cavity, pit."[74] Using this derivation, then, we see that the "witch" of Endor made use of a pit in practicing her mantic arts. This put her in a religio-historical context which extends from the Sumerians and the Babylonians in the southeast to the Greeks and, at least later, even to the Romans in the west.

Thus in the twelfth tablet of the *Gilgamesh Epic*, whose prototype goes back to the Sumerian era, it is told how Enkidu descended into the underworld to retrieve the possessions of Gilgamesh that had fallen down there, and in so doing he himself is seized by the eternal imprisonment of the realm of the dead. After Gilgamesh's importunate plea, the god Ea intervened and persuaded the lord of the underworld, Nergal, who together with his consort Ereshkigal rules the dead, to allow the spirit of Enkidu to ascend back to the earth through a hole. To his master and friend he appeared like a breath of wind, in order to communicate to him the order that prevails in the underworld.[75] The suspicion that this pit has something to do with a special ritual procedure in the conjuring up of the deceased is obvious. We find confirmation of the suspicion when we turn to the scene from the great Nekyia in the *Odyssey*. Released by Circe, the cunning Odysseus had set out on the voyage over the Oceanus to the misty realm on the shore of which the underworld opened, in order to inquire about his return home from the spirit of the blind Theban seer Teiresias, whom alone the queen of the underworld, Persephone, had allowed to keep his consciousness (*Odyssey* X.490 ff). Thus Homer has him relate to his host among the Phaeacians:

> When I had prayed sufficiently to the dead, I cut the throats of the two sheep and let the blood run into the trench, whereon the ghosts came trooping up from Erebus—brides, young bachelors, old men worn out with toil, maids who had been crossed in love, and brave men who had been killed in battle, with their armor still smirched with blood; they came from every quarter and flitted around the trench with a strange kind of screaming sound that made me turn pale with fear. (XI.34 ff)

Perhaps we recall that the first to ascend out of Erebus were the yet-unburied Elpenor and then the soul of Teiresias. The spirit of the young man is still in possession of his consciousness because, not having been buried, he has not yet come to his rest. In the case of the seer Teiresias, the situation is at first other than the poet would have preferred; for he demands to be allowed to drink of the blood of the sacrifice before he will give his prophecy (XI.95-96). Only with the draught of blood do the spirits of the dead regain their consciousness that had disappeared when they had entered into the realm of the dead. And now we know how we have to complete the picture of the nocturnal scene at Endor. And perhaps we also recall the touching scene in which Odysseus tries three times to embrace the soul of his mother that has likewise ascended out of the depths, and she each time eludes his grasp, so that he wonders whether Persephone is deceiving him with a phantom. But the spirit of his mother instructs him thus: "All people are like this when they are dead. The sinews no longer hold the flesh and bones together; these perish in the fierceness of consuming fire as soon as life has left the body, and the soul flits away as though it were a dream" (XI.218 ff).[76]

Certainly Israel rejected the practice of cremation. But the conception of the soul can hardly be distinguished from that which we encounter here in Greek poetry. Even in antiquity people were convinced that this conception of the soul could be traced back to vivid appearances of deceased persons.[77] But the passage that was just cited from the Homeric Nekyia provides sufficient evidence that the two, phantom and appearance of the dead, are indeed comparable but yet distinct from each other. In view of the troublesome character of this conception, one will rather have to think of the appearances of the dead as such along the lines that Plato assumes in the *Phaedo*, about the souls that have not yet been laid to rest in the vicinity of their monuments and burial places; he confirms this with the assertion that here "are seen all sorts of shadowy appearances of souls" (81D).[78] Thus we may regard the soul of the departed as a shadowy, intangible, and according to our conception the practically immaterial double of the living person, which, once it has entered into the underworld, can be disturbed from its unconscious slumber only in extraordinary circumstances. The ancient poets strove to maintain this character of the double by describing it as a shadow.[79]

At this point, the reader may have been struck by a twofold impression: first, that we can concretize the conception of the soul which evidently was held even by the Israelites, only by reaching out to draw religio-historical parallels; and second, that up to this point we have adduced some characterizations of the spirits of the dead as soothsaying spirits, but not a single one yet of the spirits of the dead as such. In the former fact, we are faced with the peculiar reserve of the Old Testament with respect to the realm of the dead; we shall later deal with this reserve in specific terms. And perhaps the difficulty in giving an unequivocal answer to the question of how the Israelites characterized the souls of the dead is connected with this same reserve. In the vicinity of Yahweh, the hereafter was unimportant. So far as I can see, there is not a single passage in the Old Testament where the future of man after death becomes a matter for consideration for its own sake, but only in the context of the limitations of the present life and its relationship to God.[80] The key passages on Old Testament anthropology simply do not have an answer to the question as to the special name for the souls of the dead. If one looks at Genesis 2:7, Ecclesiastes 12:7, and Psalm 104:29-30, one can get the impression that Israel indeed only distinguished between the body that is vivified by God's breath and the body that has been abandoned by God's breath and therefore has fallen into decay; there is no recognition of a third entity that maintains one's personal identity. According to Genesis 2:7, the man that was formed "out of the dust of the earth" became a "living soul" (nephesh hayyah) by Yahweh's breathing into him the "breath of life" (nishmat hayyim). In this connection the word that is rendered as "breath" appears actually to have meant "puffing, blowing,"[81] while the one translated as "soul" appears to have initially signified the throat in motion, and at a no-longer-documentable interim stage, probably also "breath."[82] The concrete connection of life to the breath led, among the Semites as well as among the Greeks with their talk about the psyche, to the addition of the meaning "life-principle, person, self, soul" to the basic meaning of the "(throat) breath." The German word Seele (English "soul") has a history that an uninitiated person could not read from it. It is said to be connected with the word See (English "sea") and thus to be a late final echo of an ancient mythological view of the sojourn of the spirits before birth and after death in certain seas or lakes.[83] When a man has drawn his last breath, he is dead (Job 11:20).[84]

In Homer, the "psyche" is the breath of life that leaves man at the moment of death, which then goes to Hades and continues to live there as the deceased being "psyche" (Iliad XVI.856). Since the "psyche," understood as breath, likewise leaves the person who faints (Iliad V. 696; Odyssey XXIV.348), the "breath-soul" evidently is understood here as an independent entity, to which—at least so long as the self-consciousness is found in the body—it is natural to attribute the experience of unconsciousness and the incapacity of the body it has left to react to anything.[85] May we draw the same conclusion in the context of Old Testament anthropology and consider that at death the "breath-soul" goes to the underworld as a "dead soul"? Opposing this conclusion, at least apparently, is the fact that, according to Ecclesiastes 12:7, after a man's death

> the dust must return to the earth, as it was,[86]
> but the breath (*ruach*) returns to God who gave it.

And correspondingly it is said in the worship of Psalm 104:29-30:

> When thou hidest thy face, they are dismayed;
>   when thou takest away their breath, they die
>   and return to their dust.
> When thou sendest forth thy Spirit, they are created;
>   and thou renewest the face of the ground (RSV).

Thus it appears here as though man consists solely of the breath-soul, as the divine and divinely bestowed life-principle, and the body. But when we remember what we have said about the reserve of the Hebrew with respect to the realm of the dead in the context of his God,[87] we begin to be cautious. And hence we have to note that in Ecclesiastes 12:7 and in Psalm 104:29-30 the subject is not the "breath-soul" (*nephesh*) but the breath in another sense (*ruach*), a word, which like its Greek equivalent "pneuma," originally denotes the breath of wind and then the spirit. If we look once again to the story of Elijah's raising of the son of the widow of Sarepta,[88] our attention is drawn to the fact that there the soul (*nephesh*) of the boy must return so that he can become alive again (1 Kings 17:21-22). And finally, Psalm 30:3 must be taken into account, where a person who has been healed thanks Yahweh for his deliverance and confesses:[89]

> O Lord, thou hast brought up my soul from Sheol,
> restored me to life from among those gone down to the
> Pit.[90]   (RSV)

Of course, one can avoid the conclusion that "soul" (*nephesh*) denoted, with reference to the deceased, the spirit of the dead, by assuming in 1 Kings 17:21-22 the meaning of "breath" and in Psalm 30:3 the meaning of "myself," but it must be asked whether this is required. The synthesis, that Yahweh vivifies the "souls" by means of his "breath," is, in any case, not ruled out.

The Hebrew could indeed actually understand the "soul" (*nephesh*) to mean the soul of the deceased, and at least later did understand it in this way. This is attested by two texts from a writing of the third century B.C. at the latest, but probably from an earlier date, inserted into his work by the author of the Enochite "Book of the Watchmen"[91] in Enoch 6–19[92]. These are Enoch 9:3 and 13:6. Enoch 9:3 speaks of the "souls [of the dead]" of all the children of men (naphshoth bene 'anasha'), and 13:6 of the "souls [of the dead]" (naphshoth) of the fallen angels.[93] The author of the "Book of the Watchmen" himself, on the other hand, in his portrayal of the intermediate state after death and before the last judgment, speaks, with respect to the individual, of the "spirit of the dead man" (ruach-'enash met, Enoch 22:5),[94] and with respect to all the dead of the "souls of all the children of men" (naphshoth kol bene 'anasha', Enoch 22:3).[95] In later Judaism the divine breath and the soul of the dead were no longer distinguished; this is shown by a passage in the book of Fourth Ezra, which presumably arose in the last third of the first century A. D. [96] Its Jewish author interprets the basic anthropological passage in Ecclesiastes 12:7, which says that at death the breath (ruach) of man returns to God,[97] with a personal understanding of the breath as the spirit of man, to mean that after the death of a man his spirit must appear in the presence of the glory of the Most High and worship him. This is the first time the fate of the spirits is differentiated before the final judgment (cf 4 Ezra 7:78 ff).[98]

The reader may be bored by these detailed bits of evidence. However, for the discussion of what is legitimate, biblically grounded thinking and believing, they possess a greater significance than may be seen in them at first glance. For some decades there has been a cherished hypothesis in theology that says that according to the Old Testament perspective, with a person's death it is all over. Even though it is a conception belonging exclusively to the Christian faith that one must think of a complete annihilation of man in death, without any surviving remnant and a corresponding completely new creation of man at the last day,[99] it must be maintained that the conception of an intermediate state after death could develop organically on the basis of the Old Testament belief about death and the soul, whatever outside influences may have contributed to this development. Otherwise there would be no comprehensible context for the New Testament parable of the rich man and poor Lazarus (Luke 16:19 ff), the saying that the same Gospel attributes to Jesus on the cross, addressed to one of the two thieves, "Verily, verily, I say to you, today you will be with me in Paradise" (Luke 23:43), or the New Testament's testimony to the Resurrection itself.

Before we turn to Israel's conceptions of the underworld, we must consider the name of *Rephaim* that is occasionally given to the spirits of the departed. Here it will become evident that no further historical dynamic issued from this name. In the Old Testament historical books it was, oddly enough, used for a pre-Israelite people who are sometimes located in the land west of the Jordan, and sometimes east of the Jordan (cf, e g, Gen. 15:20 with 14:5). And finally, these Rephaim are identified with the giants (cf, eg, Deut. 2:11; 3:11; 2 Sam. 21:16 ff). In the poetic and prophetic literature, on the other hand, the word always signifies the spirits of the dead in Sheol, in the underworld.[100] This corresponds to the usage in the Phoenician and Punic inscriptions.[101]

This peculiar state of affairs has never yet been explained. One can at best only surmise that the Rephaim, as the giants who had lived in the much earlier time, had long since died out and therefore had been given the same name as the deceased. But even so, it still remains remarkable that this name was attached to an entire people. Perhaps there is also reflected in this the fact that people had no more perception of the formation and original meaning of this word, presumably taken over from the Canaanites, than we have, as a rule, with respect to our own word "soul."[102] Some texts, unfortunately preserved only in very fragmentary form, from Ugarit and dating from the second half of the second millennium before Christ, cast some additional light on the problem. Here the Rephaim appear to be helping and healing ancestral spirits. And thus the name very well may have remained in the Hebrew language as a survival from an earlier stage of religion; in that stage of development, the deceased still were able to exercise a direct influence in the realm of the living and were not yet so hermetically sealed off in their own realm from the world of the living as appears later to have been the case and, if we take into account the Aqhat epic, was already the case among the north-Syrian Ugaritic people.[103]

In taking note of the reference given above to the possibilities of development found in the Old Testament beliefs about

the dead, we must not fail to realize that in the actual Israelite
period the underworld, though not regarded as a hell, was
likewise by no means a heaven. The views of this "land of no
return" (cf Job 7:9-10)[104] were no more appealing in Israel than
they had been for the Greeks. Thus the saying attributed to
Achilles in the *Odyssey* (XI.487 ff): "Say not a word in death's
favor; I would rather be a paid servant in a poor man's house and
be above ground than king of kings among the dead."

This characteristic utterance finds its corresponding senti-
ment in the proverb appropriated by Koheleth, which we have
already considered, that a living dog is better than a dead lion
(Eccles. 9:4).[105] In fact, there appears to have been a common
conception of the underworld that prevailed from Mesopotamia
all the way to Greece, whose roots are to be sought at the very
latest in the third millennium before Christ, and probably reach
back at least another one or two thousand years into the soil of
history. As far as we can see, it is only Egypt that, thanks to its
special religious view that has an exalted place for the sun,
distinguishes itself in its conceptions of the underworld from
those of the Aegean and western Asiatic territory.[106]

What we are able to collect from the Old Testament by way
of allusions, thanks to the reserve that we have already noted
with reference to the realm of the dead, can be grasped in more
concentrated form in the Ugaritic texts, although in this
connection also the unfortunate gaps in the texts and difficulties
in translation emerge. In the great epic of the fortunes of the
storm and weather god Baal, there are some episodes which, in
the context of what we know from the texts of the surrounding
cultures, provide an illuminating total picture. Down below, in
an abyss in the earth,[107] sits the god Mot, Death,[108] on his
throne in his city that is known as "Mire" or "Filth,"[109] as ruler
of the dead.[110] One reached the realm of the dead through a
tunnel from the two distant western hills of the sunset,
Tharguzi and Tharumagi.[111] That on the way thither one had to
cross the sea and the water of death, as we know from
Babylonian and Greek mythology, is all the more illuminating
since Ugarit itself lay only a few kilometers east of the coast.
What is said about the city of slime and mire is reminiscent of
Homer's "decaying house of Hades" that one reached after

crossing the Oceanus, at the swirling abyss in which the waters of Acheron were mingled with those of the fiery stream Pyriphlegethon, the Styx, and the Cocytus.[112] And, recalling the ferryman Urshanabi, who transported Gilgamesh over the waters of death,[113] we wonder whether the Canaanites too did not have their own Charon, whom we meet elsewhere in ancient literature only at the rivers of the underworld, but who originally appears, like Urshanabi, to have transported the souls of the deceased across the great waters into the beyond.[114]

The love for early oriental and ancient mythology appears to be playing a trick on us. For what does all this have to do with the conceptions of the underworld in the Old Testament? But caution is to be urged here. First of all, it is certain that in Israel the realm of the dead, Sheol, was thought of as a huge pit or cistern.[115] Realistically, and indeed not without a sideglance at the tomb, people occasionally spoke of the "place of destruction," Abaddon.[116] And this "pit" understandably is filled with mud and slime (Ps. 40:2). We are reminded of the conception of the underworld as a city by what is said about the "gates of death" in Psalm 9:13 and Job 38:17. One can also speak periphrastically of the "gates of darkness" (Job 38:17), and of the underworld in general as the "land of shadows and darkness" (Job 10:21). There seems always to be the river that the soul has to cross on its journey into the underworld (Job 33:18),[117] and between the "land of the living" (Ps. 52:5; Job 28:13) and the "land of the dead" (Isa. 26:19) there are great waters (2 Sam. 22:17), into whose depths the dying person sinks (Jon. 2:7; Ps. 69:2); all this suggests the temptation to construe the way of the soul to its goal as crossing the sea and passing through the maelstrom of the streams of the underworld. Of course one cannot be certain on details about to what extent the conception of the underworld as a huge, water-filled, muddy cistern has acquired an independent status in such allusions, since in mythical thinking, in any given case things can be viewed only in terms of the aspect that is immediately relevant and without any consideration for other contexts and aspects.[118] While the translator of the book of Job into Greek may have been influenced by the stories about Cerberus and other legendary creatures from the mouth of hell, still it is worthy of mention that he speaks (Job 38:17) of the watchmen of Hades. And finally, the figure that we would least have expected in the Old Testament, the ruler of the underworld, the "king of terrors" (Job 18:14), is not absent; he is death, who is strong (Song 8:6) and insatiable (Hab. 2:5).

Yet, immediately to relativize the picture once again, we must remember that in Canaanite mythology, death could become the personified underworld and, conversely, in the Old Testament the underworld could become the personification of death. In the dry season that begins in the late springtime, Baal was supposed to have left his cloud-palace and in his body to have descended through the jaws of death that were opened up to heaven.[119] And conversely, in the Old Testament Sheol, the underworld, opens up its greedy (Isa. 5:14; Hab. 2:5) and insatiable maw (Prov. 27:20; 30:16). Its unrelenting harshness (Song 8:6) does not allow the possibility of any pact with death (Isa. 28:15, 18); sooner or later, every man's turn will come.

It is only natural to raise the question of how the idea arose of a realm of the dead situated beneath the earth. This question was already a concern of Cicero's. And, not so very different from modern scholarship, he made the practice of burial in the earth the presupposition of the idea.[120] In the meantime, a more precise and more cautious perspective has been achieved by bringing into consideration the burial arrangement of deep-hewn graves and the isolation of burial places from settlements as contributing to the idea.[121] In order to understand this line of argument, one must be aware that up to the Neolithic or Late Stone Age the conception of the so-called "living corpse," which still required provisions and which could be beneficial or injurious to those left behind, was still the dominant idea.[122] In any case this is given as explanation of the fact that at that time people buried their dead within the house or at least in the farmstead or the area of the settlement; in this way the deceased were given a share in the place of residence and the household goods.[123] At the time when people began to position the bodies of the dead facing west, toward the setting sun, the idea of the realm of the dead or of access to the subterranean land of the dead in the west appears already to have been present.[124] The emergence of this idea is easily explained from the assumed subterranean course of the sun as it corresponds to the natural human perspective.[125] And thus also we understand how, wherever a great sea in the west was known, the entrance to this realm of the dead was perceived to lie beyond the sea. And we also suspect that the fiery stream that is supposed to empty into its depths was derived from the fiery reflection on the sea at sunset. Since the orientation of burials to the west in the cultural sphere of western Asia can be demonstrated in one case about the year 6000 B.C. and even before the separation of place of residence and place of burial,[126] it is natural to ask whether this already attests such advanced belief about the deceased. If one also takes into account the similar orientation of a skeleton from the Early Stone Age family cemetery at La Ferrassie in the Dordogne, a significantly earlier emergence of the conception is not ruled out;[127] of course one must also keep in mind that here we are dealing with a single find from such an early time. If the emphasis is placed upon the separation of house or settlement and burial place, it must be remembered that apart from occasional exceptions, for example in Ugarit,[128] this separation took place in the area between Hindu-Kush and the Aegean between 5500 and 4000 B.C.[129] Thus in any case, we may reckon with the fact that since that time, the conception of the underworld prevailed in the Aegean–western Asian region. Of course one will be obliged to regard the conception of a soul of the deceased one as the presupposition of this conception of the underworld, not as its consequence. We have already established that its origin cannot be separated from the corresponding phenomena and appearances which strike contemporary man as extraordinary and unbelievable.[130]

Having reached this point in our reflections, we are necessarily confronted with the question whether the belief in a realm of the dead situated in the west and the further belief, which presumably followed the other at some distance in time, in a subterranean realm of the dead that is accessible in the west, are not the presupposition rather than the result of an altered burial custom.

It is obvious that this belief must necessarily have had as its consequence the conception of a journey of the deceased person.[131] In order for this departed person actually to reach his goal, he required, on the one hand, a "proper" burial,[132] and on the other hand, the necessary provisions for the long journey. Otherwise he would be condemned to restless wandering, scraping food from others' pots and gathering scraps of sustenance on the streets, as Enkidu pictures it to his friend Gilgamesh, when he asked him:

Did you see one whose spirit is not cared for?—
I saw this too: The remnants of food in the pot, the scraps lying on the street, this is his fare![133]

If one may interpret the furnishings of the tomb in this sense as food and other provisions of everyday needs for the journey of the deceased,[134] in view of the fact that in Israelite tombs also there was no lack of provisions of food and drink, and of the fact that there was concern not to bury a person naked,[135] one may conclude that the idea of such a journey of the deceased person was not foreign to Israel. With reference to these furnishings of the tombs it would be better not to speak of sacrifices for the dead.[136] However, it is no more possible here to count on thorough-going consistency than with the other conceptions that have to do with the hereafter. And therefore, so long as it is a matter of the provision of food, ornaments, weapons, and clothing that are placed in the tomb, it is difficult to determine how much of a role is played in this provisioning of the dead by the conception of the "living corpse," which as far as feeling is concerned, still prevails even down to the present when one views the body of a familiar person who has died.[137]

In the history of human consciousness, earlier conceptions that belong to a stage that in and of itself has already been outgrown still survive with tenacity and enter into the most peculiar combinations with the pattern of thought that has, in the meantime, come to prevail. This is nowhere so clearly shown as in the burial customs and the beliefs concerning the dead held by the peoples. The most splendid example in the ancient world certainly is afforded by the pertinent Egyptian rites and myths. Here the fate of the corpse and the future of the deceased in the beyond are always joined; and therefore people took the well-known precautions by means of mummification, artificial heads, the Ka-statues, pyramids, burial plots, and so on, in order to insure eternal life. According to our judgment, here a primordial superstitious fear again and again demolished the beginnings of an ethical perspective on the future life, as it found its expression in the mythological formulation concerning the judgment of the dead. [138] The belief in a particular realm of the dead did not liberate men from the fear of spirits of the dead that might be injurious to them. Thus even the book of wisdom of Ani, from the time of the great pharaohs of the Eighteenth Dynasty who bore the names of Amenophes and Tutmosis, contains the counsel:

> Satisfy the spirit (of the deceased person)
>   and do what will be pleasing to him.
> Abstain from what he abhors.
> Then you will be spared from the many injuries
>   that he causes,
> For all mischief comes from him. [139]

The question as to how the spirits of the deceased could cause such trouble may be answered in terms of a Babylonian conjuration, which offers a religio-historical panorama.

> A dead man's spirit (*etimmu*)[140] has appeared,
> and is gnawing on me; may he be detached from my body,
> may he turn. . . .
> May he eat what is good, may he drink what is good,
> may he eat a little bread, may he drink something cool,
> Some water for the throat! Whether he is a strange spirit
> of a deceased one, whose name no one knows,
> Whether he is a dead man's spirit that dashes about, or
> a dead man's spirit that walks,
> or the spirit of a dead man who lies in the desert,
> or the spirit of a dead man who died in the water. . . . [141]

We break off with the recitation of the text here, because enough has been quoted to make it clear that this has reference to obvious cases where proper burial has been omitted; because the deceased person was not fittingly buried and was not given any of the usual gifts for the dead, he has perhaps become malicious. This inference may be confirmed by yet another look at the twelfth tablet of the *Gilgamesh Epic*, because there the fate of one who has been buried properly and that of a person who has been left unburied are explicitly contrasted.

> "Have you seen him who was killed in battle?"
> "I have seen him; his parents support his head, and his
>   wife weeps over him."
> "Have you seen him whose body was cast on the
>   steppe (unburied)?"
> "I have seen him; he finds no rest or peace in
>   Hades."[142]

But now having had our attention drawn to the phenomenon, we can also look to the west to discover it again, all the way from the *Iliad* to the *Aeneid*.[143] Vergil probably exhibits it most impressively in the scene at Acheron.

A grim warden guards these waters and streams, terrible in his squalor—Charon, on whose chin lies a mass of unkempt, hoary hair; his eyes are staring orbs of flame; his squalid garb hangs by the knot from his shoulders. Unaided, he poles the boat, tends the sails, and in his murky craft convoys the dead—now aged, but a god's old age is hardy and green. Hither rushed all the throng, streaming to the banks; mothers and men and bodies of high-souled heroes, their life now done, boys and unwedded girls, and sons placed on the pyre before their fathers' eyes; thick as the leaves of the forest that at autumn's first frost dropping fall, and thick as the birds that from the seething deep flock shoreward, when the chill of the year drives them overseas and sends them into sunny lands. They stood, pleading to be the first ferried across, and stretched out hands in yearning for the farther shore. But the surly boatman takes now these, now those, while others he thrusts apart, back from the brink. Then aroused and amazed by the disorder, Aeneas cries: "Tell me, O maiden, what means the crowding to the river? What seek the spirits? or by what rule do these leave the banks, and those sweep the lurid stream with oars?" To him thus briefly spake the aged priestess: "Anchises' son, true offspring of gods, thou seest the deep pools of Cocytus and the Stygian marsh, by whose power the gods fear to swear falsely. All this

crowd thou seest is helpless and graveless; yonder warden is
Charon; those whom the flood carries are the buried. Nor
may he bear them over the dreadful banks and hoarse-voiced
waters ere their bones have found a resting-place. A hundred
years they roam, and flit about these shores; then only are
they admitted and revisit the longed-for pools."

Anchises' son paused and stayed his steps, pondering
much, and pitying in soul their cruel lot.[144]

One can probably conclude that in this belief in the properly
performed burial as the precondition of admission into the
realm of the dead, at any rate the belief, carried over from the
Stone Age, about the "living corpse" still survives.[145]

When we turn, after this survey, once again to the Old
Testament, on the one hand, we very quickly become aware of
the fact that here too the conception of the "living corpse" has
entered into a combination, though to be sure a quite
distinctive one, with that of the sojourn of the soul of the
deceased in the realm of the dead that is the fate of everyone.
For while in the texts and the contexts that we have been
considering, we have encountered the interpretation of
properly performed burial as a precondition of one's transition
into the realm of the shades and found this at least among the
Greeks to be regarded as definitive, in Israel it appears to have
been regarded each on its own terms rather than as responsible
for one's fate in the underworld.[146] We can most simply
illustrate this with the example of the ideal of life that was
exemplified in the patriarchs, to die at a ripe old age after a full
life and to be gathered to one's people.[147] The significance that
pertains to the latter part of this expression is shown by a
comparison with a formula that appears in the books of Kings, a
formula that has long since lost its original meaning and has
become a euphemistic paraphrase for dying; "Then so-and-so
slept with his fathers." The fact that it no longer means burial in
the family tomb is shown, for example, by 1 Kings 14:31, where,
as with all the kings of Judah, this formula is followed by the
note, "and was buried with his fathers in the city of David."
Thus we may infer that "to be gathered to his people" and "to
sleep with his fathers" in the meantime had become an
expression of the assurance that the person who was buried in

the family tomb also would find his rest in the underworld in the company of his ancestors.[148] The importance that was placed upon actually being buried in the ancestral tomb and the significance that this held for one who was exiled point to the correspondence between the burial and one's fate in the underworld.[149] And if there was for the Israelite one single glimmer of hope connected with death, it was this: to continue even in death to be included in the tribal bond, bodily and as a spirit.[150]

From the perspective afforded by this presupposition it is understandable that for the Israelite as well as for other men of antiquity it was the most severe punishment imaginable for one to be denied a fitting burial, his rest in the tomb to be disturbed, his body or his bones to be destroyed. Correspondingly, it was the most serious threat of punishment imaginable when the prophet Jeremiah predicted to the king Jehoiakim that he would have the burial of an ass.

> Therefore thus says the Lord concerning Jehoiakim the son
> of Josiah, king of Judah:
> They shall not lament for him, saying,
>   'Ah my brother!' or 'Ah sister!'[151]
> They shall not lament for him, saying,
>   'Ah lord!' or 'Ah his majesty!'
> With the burial of an ass he shall be buried,
>   dragged and cast forth beyond the gates of Jerusalem."
>   (Jer. 22:18-19 RSV)

What this meant in realistic terms is set forth in Jeremiah 36:30: "His corpse will be exposed to the heat by day and to the frost by night." In the Orient an ass was not, and is not, buried; at best it is thrown upon the large refuse heap outside the city, or it is simply allowed to lie there where it has expired. If we may trust the testimony of the neighboring Phoenicians, the person who was not buried could not enter the underworld.[152] And undoubtedly this testimony would best be fitted into the framework of the western Asian-Aegean belief about the deceased. However, Isaiah 14:4 ff will show us that this conception may not be extended, at least not without

limitations, to Israel as well.[153] According to Israelite belief, a
special fate also awaited those who as miscarriages, uncircumcised men, executed persons, orphans, and even unwanted and
despised slaves were cast into the large common grave outside
the gates of the city, the "grave of the children of the people" (cf
Jer. 26:23; Job 3:16; 2 Kings 23:6),[154] an arrangement which
ancient Rome also, for example, had.[155] To die uncircumcised
or on the way to execution was regarded as especially shameful
and dishonorable. This is evident in the threat against the king
of Tyre, which reaches its climactic point in the announcement
that he will die the death of the uncircumcised (Ezek. 28:10; cf
also 31:18).[156] This by no means simply signified an end in a
common grave, but also a corresponding association in the
underworld; this is shown by the lamentation over "Egypt's
descent into hell" in Ezekiel 32:19-28.[157] Here it is prophesied
that Egypt, as well as Assyria, Elam, Meshech, and Tubal, in
contrast to the heroes of earlier times, who were buried in
honor and in honor went into the underworld, would suffer the
fate of the uncircumcised and those who were executed. All
these must remain in the underworld in the very same
dishonorable company into which their corpses had been
cast.[158]

Moreover, the disturbance of one's rest in the tomb
signified more than an act sentimentally regarded as impiety
and concernedly viewed as an offense against the respect owed
to the mortal remains of a man as an end in itself. It is
self-evident that this fate could be used as a prophetic threat (cf
Jer. 8:1). It is equally obvious that it could appear in grave and
sarcophagus inscriptions in Phoenicia as well as in Jerusalem
among imprecations and curses, and could be practiced as
political punishment against the tombs of the kings of a
conquered people.[159] And in fact it is specifically declared in
one Assyrian royal inscription that the opening of the crypt, the
exposure of the bones, and their ultimate removal to the land of
the victor would disturb the rest of the spirits of the dead.[160]
Hence one may ask whether the destruction of the corpse by
dogs (1 Kings 21:23; 2 Kings 9:3 ff),[161] its being burned (Josh.
7:25), and even the burning of bones taken from their tomb
(Amos 2:1) would likewise have as a consequence an assault

upon the rest of the underworld or a destruction of the souls of the deceased. At any rate, Amos saw in this an offense that God would punish by burning the cities of the culprits (Amos 2:1 ff). According to Old Testament belief, a punishment that reaches beyond this present life is not allowed to men.[162] This also serves to explain the fact that in Judaism the burial of a dead person was regarded as a work pleasing to God (Tob. 1:21).[163]

In the only scene from the underworld preserved for us in the Old Testament, we once more encounter, in a most impressive expression, the distinctiveness of the Israelite belief concerning the dead with its correspondence between the fate of the corpse and the fate in the realm of the dead. We refer to the song of ridicule over the fall of the world-ruler in the guise of the morning star that has fallen from heaven to earth (Isa. 14:4b ff). We begin our quotation with the second strophe, which lets us observe the reaction of the mighty ones among the spirits, who have been shaken from their eternal slumber by the triumphant upheaval of the underworld.

> Sheol beneath is stirred up
> to meet you when you come,
> it rouses the shades[164] to greet you,
> all who were leaders of the earth;
> it raises from their thrones
> all who were kings of the nations.
> All of them will speak
> and say to you:
> "You too have become as weak as we!
> You have become like us!"
> Your pomp is brought down to Sheol,
> the sound of your harps;
> maggots are the bed beneath you,
> and worms are your covering.
> (Isa. 14:9-11 RSV)

The reader will ask, "Is the underworld actually identical with the grave, in the mind of the poet?" The following strophe shows that the ruler has actually arrived in Sheol.

How you are fallen from heaven,
  O Day Star, son of Dawn!
How you are cut down to the ground,
  you who laid the nations low!
You said in your heart,
  "I will ascend to heaven;
above the stars of God
  I will set my throne on high;
I will sit on the mount of assembly
  in the far north;
I will ascend above the heights of the clouds,
  I will make myself like the Most High."
But you are brought down to Sheol,
  to the depths of the pit.
                    (Isa. 14:12-15 RSV)

Thus, down there in the dark underworld where it is utterly
dark, and far from all who have been buried in honor, the
world-tyrant finds his grave, because, as the concluding verses
of the third strophe tell us, he, different from the other kings of
the nations, has been

cast out, away from your sepulchre,
  like a loathed untimely birth,[165]
clothed with the slain, those pierced by the sword,[166]
  who go down to the stones of the Pit,
  like a dead body trodden under foot.
                    (Isa. 14:19 RSV)[167]

IV. Yahweh and the dead

**For in death there is no remembrance of thee;
in Sheol who can give thee praise?**
                    (Ps. 6:5 RSV)

In a dispute with the Sadducees, who as conservative
theologians denied the resurrection of the dead, Jesus'

opponents thought they had driven him into a corner. In response he cited a passage that stressed the identity of the God who had revealed himself to the patriarchs with the God who made himself known to Moses at the burning bush: "I am the God of Abraham, the God of Isaac, and the God of Jacob" (Exod. 3:6). This offered clear scriptural testimony that for none of the fathers, and thus also for no other man, had God withdrawn himself, nor would he withdraw himself, in death. He cited his scriptural proof with the words, "God is not the God of the dead, but of the living" (Matt. 12:26-27).[168] Underlying this offering of proof from Scripture, in addition to his own experience and assurance of faith, there is a certain under-standing of Scripture that arises out of the fact that the Scripture as a whole, besides being the revelation, in the Law, of the will of God for Israel, is in essence prophecy. It was apparently in circles that held this conviction that the prophetic books received their final form, the Psalms were correspondingly revised, and in addition several writings arose, which later, except for the book of Daniel, were refused acceptance into the rabbinical canon and were incorporated into the Alexandrian Greek canon only in select parts. Today they form a part of the books which are counted as the Apocrypha in the Protestant churches, and in the Catholic churches as a component of the Old Testament; and finally and especially, the so-called Pseudepigrapha, writings that circulated under the name, or as the account of the life, suffering, or death, of a noted hero of the faith.[169] Actually the boundary between the canonical books, which provide the foundation for obligatory doctrine, and the noncanonical books is a fluid one; yet on the whole we must acknowledge that the Jewish and Christian fathers who were responsible for making the official collections possessed a theological sensitivity of a high quality.

It is not our purpose in developing this bit of the history of biblical literature to prompt the Protestant churches to reconsider their decision in favor of the Hebrew Old Testament canon and against the Greek. Instead, we intend to awaken a historical sensitivity to the fact that there is a difference between those of the postexilic period who, according to our present-day perspective, remained rooted in the writings from the time of Israel's kings and the beliefs of that time, on the one hand, and on the other hand, the intellectual and spiritual world in which Jesus grew up. We must be aware of this when in the following the relationship of Yahweh to the deceased is spoken of, and in that connection Jesus' assertion is given a sense that is contrary to his belief, that the God of Israel was in fact first of all the God of the living and not of the dead. God was mightier in Jesus' view than in the view of his early ancestors. Hence for him he was also the God of the dead.

The creation narrative in Genesis 1, which goes back to the ancient tradition, is so harmonious in its arrangement and so stately in its formal language that we do not even notice how there is nothing said in it either about the making of chaos or about the creation of the underworld. And thus it corresponds to the ancient Israelite belief! The God who rides upon the wind and sits enthroned in the heavens (Ps. 104:3; 33:13-14) is the Lord of this bright world that encompasses heaven and earth; and as such he is king over the whole earth (Ps. 47:7). But he is not therefore also the king of the underworld. Such an assertion might well have appeared to the Israelites at the time of the monarchy and of early Judaism as monstrous as would the statement to a Greek that Zeus was the king of the underworld, or to a Canaanite the same concerning Baal, or to a Babylonian concerning Marduk-Bel. [170]

The Greeks told that the three sons of Kronos, Zeus, Poseidon, and Hades, had divided their patrimony. In that division, the heavens fell Zeus' lot, the ocean going to Poseidon and the underworld to Hades. Only the earth and the mountain of the gods, Olympus, were to be open to all on an equal basis. But even here the predominance of Zeus prevailed de facto over the earth (*Iliad* XV. 185 ff). [171] It should be noted that as the god of the heavens Zeus possessed the preeminence, but not sole lordship; superior power, but not omnipotence. [172] And at first it was not otherwise even with Yahweh, though we do not need to obscure the differences that at once become evident. The Canaanites, from whom presumably the Israelites borrowed a number of their beliefs, knew no dividing up of the world among their gods such as the *Iliad* had, but they did know a struggle among the gods over the dominion over the earth, manifested in the changing of the seasons of the year: the storm-god Baal, according to this view, had to defend himself against the attacks of the sea-god Jam and finally had to follow the king of the underworld, Mot, into his dark and gloomy kingdom.[173] After his worshipers became established in Canaan, Yahweh drew to himself the sphere of lordship that had belonged to Baal and thereby became the victor over the rebellious sea (cf Ps. 93:2 ff; 24:1-2; Job 38:8 ff). Since he presumably had earlier moved into the role of the Creator God and the Father of the gods and men, El (= "God"), he necessarily stood, in contrast to Baal, above the play of the forces of nature; the divine victory was traced back to the beginnings of creation, and the originally divine elements ultimately became the mere material of his creative activity.[174] But just as this seizure and development of power over the Canaanite cosmos by the God who came from Sinai required some time, so also further steps were required before he also would cast down from his throne the "king of terrors" (Job 18:14), in order to become now in fact the God of the living and the dead, a development in which the dead themselves necessarily were transformed.

When Amos 9:2 and Psalm 139:8 emphasize the impossibility of hiding from God, either in heaven or in the underworld, it still remains doubtful, in view of this play with what are for man impossible possibilities, whether it has reference to more than the impossibility for man during his lifetime to escape the lordship of God.[175] One aspect of this impossibility, of course, is the fact that Yahweh has the life and death of man at his disposal. This is said in another way in a confession, which in an expanded horizon is capable of an expansion of meaning, with respect to his holding sway over men's destiny; he is the one who "kills and brings to life; he brings down to Sheol and raises up" (1 Sam. 2:6 RSV).

And yet, to transpose this quotation into terms of our own understanding of the world, what is in mind is not an action related to the deceased, but rather one related to a man whose life is in danger. Here once again we encounter the conception that is distinctive in Israel, that the person who is grievously ill or in mortal danger is already entangled in the snares of death or has already gone into the underworld (cf Ps. 116:3,8; 18:4-5, 16-17).[176] No one but Yahweh decides whether the sick person will be healed, the prisoner freed, the persecuted delivered, or whether they must die; for it is he who delivers man to death (Job 30:23). But at first this power of decision over life and death no more makes him the Lord of the underworld than Zeus, whose corresponding authority finds its expression in the symbol of the scales. Thus we read in the *Iliad* XXII.208 ff, in the episode of Achilles' pursuit of Hector, who has been strengthened by Apollo:

> But when for the fourth time they were come to the springs, lo then the Father lifted on high his golden scales, and set therein two fates of grievous death, one for Achilles, and one for horse-taming Hector; then he grasped the balance by the midst and raised it; and down sank the day of doom of Hector, and departed unto Hades; and Phoebus Apollo left him.[177]

Did not Yahweh's power extend farther than this? We recall the verses that were later inserted into the Job-poem, which in exaltation of his wisdom and power tell of his gaze that pierces earth and waters and extends into the underworld, before which gaze even the spirits of the dead[178] tremble (Job 26:5 ff). But this may well be, like Amos 9:2 and Psalm 139:8, a statement about boundaries. Still maintained is the line that separates the God who clothes himself in light like a garment (Ps. 104:2) from the place of concentrated impurity.

Since the deceased person belonged to the underworld, and had fallen victim to the king of terrors, contact with a corpse would contaminate an Israelite and thereby render him incapable of participating in religious ceremonies.[179] In this context one may also call to mind, by way of illuminating the relationship between Yahweh and the deceased, the parting words that Euripides puts in the mouth of the godess Artemis just before the death of her favorite, Hippolytus. Certainly there is here a closeness between gods and men that would have appeared dangerous to the Old Testament, which so carefully maintains the distance between God and creature. Yet this closeness could rise to lofty heights, as is attested in the *Iliad*: thus the terse remarks concerning Zeus, who cannot avert the fate of death of his son Sarpedon, heeding the objection of Hera, who points to the order that Zeus himself has guaranteed: "The sire of gods and men gave assent to her words. But he scattered drops of blood earthward in honor of his beloved son, who was to fall to Patroclus' assault in Troy, far from the land of his fathers." Against the background of this grief and this sympathy the boundary of death that separates gods and men becomes clear in the words of Artemis:

> Farewell! I must avoid beholding the dying;
> The breath of death must not profane my eye,
> And the hateful moment is not far away.[180]

To the Christian who regards the "Father, into thy hands I commend my spirit" as the option that is obviously open to him and explicitly commanded for him,[181] this may sound dreadful, but it nevertheless remains characteristic of large segments of ancient religion.[182] Death draws the boundary line between the gods and the men who are devoted to them and serve them. When in dying they fall into profound unconsciousness, they also are removed, even for Israel, from the realm of Yahweh's dominion; they are "uninteresting" to him, and have become unsuited for the purpose of spreading the rule of God and fellowship with God as the fulfillment of his creative and redemptive intention.[183]

Since the God who enters upon a history with mankind does not propose to achieve this purpose without man's response in open praise and exaltation of his deeds, and it is this praise and exaltation that will alone reveal the character of these deeds as *his* deeds,[184] the God of Israel is simply dependent upon the praise of Israel as well as the individual Israelite. Therefore the individual in his distress can remind him of the loss that the person's premature death would cause him. Thus the suppliant in Psalm 30:9 (RSV) asks him:

> What profit is there in my death,
> if I go down to the Pit?

> Will the dust praise thee?
> Will it tell of thy faithfulness?

And one who has been stricken with grievous sufferings from the days of his youth onward appeals to him even more urgently in Psalm 88:10 ff (RSV).

> Dost thou work wonders for the dead?
>   Do the shades[185] rise up to praise thee?
> Is thy steadfast love declared in the grave,
>   or thy faithfulness in Abaddon?
> Are thy wonders known in the darkness,
>   or thy saving help in the land of forgetfulness?

The answer is given in Psalm 6:5 (RSV).

> For in death there is no remembrance of thee;
> in Sheol who can give thee praise?

And in still sharper fashion, setting the living and the dead in contrast to each other and thereby at the same time calling God's attention to these his people, Psalm 115 concludes:

> The dead do not praise the Lord,
>   nor do any that go down into silence.
> But we will bless the Lord
>   from this time forth and for evermore.
>   (vv 17-18 RSV)

V. The bitterness of death

> **My God, my God, why hast thou forsaken me!**
>   **(Ps. 22:1)**

During our youth the fact that we must die remains for us strangely unreal. Even when one is directly affected through the loss of a person who is beloved, or when in observing the death of a contemporary, one becomes aware of the possibility of dying here and now, still this remains peculiarly theoretical. Even in times of war one counts on one's own chances of survival. The few decades granted to man at best, which can be surveyed by the mind, appear practically unlimited, and the end is remotely distant. Even though in this respect man in a certain sense always remains an illusionist, yet things do change when he reaches his forties. In any case the midpoint has been passed. And under the impact of increasing demands of work and family, the weeks, months, and years seem to go by ever more rapidly. The finiteness of the lifespan that is allotted to us comes into view less sentimentally than when we were eighteen and imperiously demands that we ultimately come to terms with ourselves and our plans. Yearning for rejuvenation and a new beginning, secret envy of the young, whom the same destiny awaits after all as awaited their ancestors, calm resignation, and an austere readiness to depart, all can follow each other in succession. Moreover, one's feelings with regard to advancing age, on the one hand yearned for and on the other hand feared, are subject to change; for this age can bring fulfillment to us as well as loneliness and disfigurement.

Earlier we remarked, almost casually, that it was the Israelite's ideal of life to die in old age after a fulfilling and satisfying life.[186] In view of the anticipated night of death, even the most troubled life must have appeared to him as far more desirable, as the *Odyssey* puts in the mouth of the ghost of Achilles.[187] "Light is sweet, and it is pleasant for the eyes to behold the sun. For if a man lives many years, let him rejoice in them all; but let him remember that the days of darkness will be many. All that comes is vanity" (Eccles. 11:7-8 RSV).

The same man perceived with keen insight the burdens of old age. He used those burdens as a basis for the admonition addressed to his pupils to enjoy their youth.

> Rejoice, O young man, in your youth, and let your heart cheer you in the days of your youth; walk in the ways of your heart and the sight of your eyes. But know that for all these things God will bring you into judgment.

Remove vexation from your mind, and put away pain from your body; for youth and the dawn of life are vanity.

Remember also your Creator in the days of your youth, before the evil days come, and the years draw nigh, when you will say, "I have no pleasure in them"; before the sun and the light and the moon and the stars are darkened and the clouds return after the rain; in the day when the keepers of the house[188] tremble, and the strong men[189] are bent, and the grinders[190] cease because they are few, and those that look through the windows[191] are dimmed, and the doors on the street are shut; when the sound of the grinding is low, and one rises up at the voice of a bird, and all the daughters of song[192] are brought low; they are afraid also of what is high, and terrors are in the way; the almond tree blossoms,[193] the grasshopper drags itself along and desire fails[194]; because man goes to his eternal home, and the mourners go about the streets; before the silver cord is snapped, or the golden bowl[195] is broken, or the pitcher is broken at the fountain, or the wheel broken at the cistern.

(Eccles. 11:9-12:6 RSV)

In view of all these experiences, a Greek could, like the aged Sophocles, draw the conclusion that it is folly to wish for too long a life; indeed, in looking back upon the struggle and trouble of a long life he could even come to the conclusion that it would be best for a man not to have been born at all.

> Anyone who scorns the middle way,
> Craving an excessive length of days,
> Him I consider to be the slave of folly;
> For the longer lifespan serves only
> To heap up misery upon woe.
> Joys—where are they,
> When a man lives on beyond a moderate span,
> Until at last the Deliverer comes
> Who sets things right for everyone,
> When the messenger of Hades extends an invitation
> To a wedding without music or dancing?
> Death is the end.
>
> Never to have been born at all:
> None can conceive a loftier thought!

And the second-best is this: once born,
Quickly to return to the dust.
Youthful folly passes away,
And already distresses have begun;
Trouble and pain,
Envy, strife, struggle, war,
And slaughter, until at last
The worst of all appears,
Helpless old age, unaccompanied
By praise, by love, or by friends,
The wretchedness of the world one's only guide.
                    Oedipus at Colonus 1213 ff

This will find its echo in Jerusalem in the third century B.C. in the Preacher in Ecclesiastes. There, witness is borne, in the thoughts on the sufferings of the oppressed that are regarded with indifference, to the strength of an indigenous tradition that is being formed in the crisis of Judaism in encounter with the hellenistic spirit.

Again I saw all the oppressions that are practiced under the sun. And behold, the tears of the oppressed, and they had no one to comfort them! On the side of their oppressors there was power, and there was no one to comfort them. And I thought the dead who are already dead more fortunate than the living who are still alive; but better than both is he who has not yet been, and has not seen the evil deeds that are done under the sun.
                    (Eccles. 4:1-3 RSV).

But in the Old Testament this is a marginal utterance of a man who in the encounter with Hellenism has learned to see the world and to evaluate it with his own eyes,[196] even though there had long been something comparable in the form of a curse pronounced upon the day of one's own birth, as an expression of deepest despair.[197]

If we may draw a conclusion from the silence of the sources, such sufferings as these, and even others, still did not allow a person voluntarily to put an end to his own life. Perhaps the Israelite too, like the Platonic Socrates, if he had been asked

the reasons for this attitude, would have remembered that
man, as the property of God, is not allowed to withdraw himself
from the service he owes to God.[198] The Israelite made at least
one exception: If a man was left with nothing but the choice
between a certain shameful death and suicide, for the sake of his
honor he had to choose the latter, whether he killed himself (1
Sam. 31:4-5; 2 Sam. 17:23; 1 Kings 16:18; cf Judg. 16:28 ff) or
had the help of his armor-bearer (Judg. 9:54).[199] One need only
recall the defenders of the mountain fortress Masada, who in
the face of the Roman conquerors first killed their women and
children and then each other;[200] telling of this, the Jewish
historians put in the mouth of the leader Eleazar the saying that
God had been gracious to them in allowing them to die well and
freely.[201]

Here the Jew interpreted the concept of honor more
narrowly than did the Greek, for whom, insofar as he was not
otherwise bound by the faith of the mysteries or by
philosophical conviction, the words of the Sophoclean Ajax
might serve.

> No noble man will strive for longer life
> When his misfortune holds no hope of change!
> What pleasure is there, when every day brings
>   death
> One step closer, then draws back half a step?
> I would not give a copper for a man
> Who warms himself on empty hopes.
> The noble person lives in honor or in honor
> Dies. This is all I have to say.
>   (Sophocles, *Ajax* 473 ff)[202]

But by the very nature of the Old Testament, this whole
realm of life is given expression there only in peripheral
fashion. It is not length of life, even though ultimately filled
with misery, but what appears to the person affected as the
altogether too brief span of life that is repeatedly lamented in
the Old Testament's pages. Psalm 90 (v. 10 RSV) has the people
as a whole bewail the transitoriness of human life which,
measured by God's eternity, is so troubling:

> The years of our life are threescore and ten,
>   or even by reason of strength fourscore;
> yet their span is but toil and trouble;
>   they are soon gone, and we fly away.

Similarly, in verse 12, the psalmist has the people cry out, in view of the divine wrath which at any time can annihilate man, who is like the grass that grows up in the morning and in the evening is withered away (v 6).

> So teach us to number our days
>   that we may get a heart of wisdom. (RSV)

The man who is conscious of his finitude and frailty, the people who are conscious of their transitoriness, are to be instructed by their weakness and to live in such a way that they do not stir their God to wrath.

And thus the suppliant of Psalm 39, who apparently had suffered frequent grave illnesses, calls on Yahweh:

> Lord, let me know my end,
>   and what is the measure of my days;
>   let me know how fleeting my life is!
> Behold, thou hast made my days a few handbreadths,
>   and my lifetime is as nothing in thy sight.
> Surely every man stands as a mere breath!
>   Surely man goes about as a shadow!
>   Surely for nought are they in turmoil;
>   man heaps up, and knows not who will gather!
> And now, Lord, for what do I wait?
>   My hope is in thee.
>   (vv 4-7 RSV)

He repeatedly emphasizes that he knows that it is Yahweh's hand of punishment that has smitten him; indeed, by means of suffering it has, like a consuming moth, destroyed the attractiveness of his body, in order that in his weakness he might entrust himself to the one who alone can help him.

> Hear my prayer, O Lord,
>   and give ear to my cry;

> hold not thy peace at my tears!
> For I am thy passing guest,
>   a sojourner, like all my fathers.
> Look away from me, that I may know gladness,
>   before I depart and be no more!
>   (vv 12-13)[203]

A life that has the span of a hand's breadth, in its transitoriness like southern grass or like a shadow—these metaphors are not meant to be understood in the context of the ages mentioned in Psalm 90:10, but from the perspective of data such as are still today reported from the developing countries and particularly from the poorest parts of Africa. As to how the life-expectancy of man appeared in Old Testament times, we may gauge this from an example which, to be sure, belongs to the New Testament era. In 1968 four tombs were excavated at Giv'at ha-Mivtar, now in the northeastern part of Jerusalem, but one time situated just outside its gates. These tombs deserve a certain melancholy notoriety because in them we have for the first time they archaeological-anthropological proof of a crucifixion.[204] They have been dated between the middle of the second century B.C. and the last third of the first century A.D. The examination of the skeletal remains of some thirty-five persons altogether shows that 54 percent of them were under twenty-five years of age, and 40 percent were older than thirty-five; only 6 percent were older than sixty years of age.[205] I think that against this background we can better understand the earnest petitions of the psalter asking the God who punishes the sins of men to be gracious to man because of his transiency. And certainly this perspective allows us to comprehend the exuberance and jubilation of those whom he has caused to be healed and whose prayer of thanksgiving might be expressed, for example, in the words of Psalm 103:

> Bless the Lord, O my soul;
>   and all that is within me,
>   bless his holy name!
> Bless the Lord, O my soul,
>   and forget not all his benefits,
> who forgives all your iniquity,

who heals all your diseases,
who redeems your life from the Pit,
who crowns you with steadfast love and mercy,
who satisfies you with good as long as you live
so that your youth is renewed like the eagle's.

The Lord works vindication
and justice for all who are oppressed.
He made known his ways to Moses,
his acts to the people of Israel.
The Lord is merciful and gracious,
slow to anger and abounding in steadfast love.
He will not always chide,
nor will he keep his anger for ever.
He does not deal with us according to our sins,
nor requite us according to our iniquities.
For as the heavens are high above the earth,
so great is his steadfast love toward those who fear him;
as far as the east is from the west,
so far does he remove our transgressions from us.
As a father pities his children,
so the Lord pities those who fear him.
For he knows our frame;
he remembers that we are dust.

As for man, his days are like grass;
he flourishes like a flower of the field;
for the wind passes over it, and it is gone,
and its place knows it no more.
But the steadfast love of the Lord is from everlasting to
everlasting
upon those who fear him,
and his righteousness to children's children,
to those who keep his covenant
and remember to do his commandments.
(vv 1-18 RSV)[206]

Is it possible for us to comprehend what pressure, in
addition to his physical suffering, was felt by a man who was
seriously ill and now had to bear not only the bodily misery but
also the misery of the soul, the torment of the piercing question
of what transgressions of God's will had brought upon him this

suffering, while at the same time his friends and kinfolk dissociated themselves from one thus visibly singled out by God, lest they similarly draw down his wrath upon themselves?[207] If illness and premature death were Yahweh's response to a man's guilt, and perhaps even to the guilt of his fathers,[208] with what remorse and bitterness then did a man look toward his end? And how often has the painful cry of a man in his youth or in the prime of life, "My God, my God, why hast thou forsaken me?" (Ps. 22:1), as it was later cited by witnesses as the last words of the Crucified One (Mark 15:34), been answered by an ugly voice: "Do you still hold fast your integrity? Curse God, and die" (Job 2:9 RSV)?

Who would deny, in a time when the connections between body and soul, the psychic and the somatic, have once again come into view, that sickness can be the result of guilt, and premature death a result of transgressions of the holy will of God? But what becomes of a man when this is turned into casuistry, and an inference is drawn from the seriousness of his sufferings and from his premature death to his corresponding proportional guilt in this life? Anyone who has ever witnessed the death of a person who is held captive by these notions knows that there is no greater bitterness in death than when one torments himself with this question: "My God, my God, *why* hast thou forsaken *me*"?

VI. The problem of Job, or "Where is the Father?"

How often is it that the lamp of
the wicked is put out,
That their calamity comes upon them?
(Job 21:17 RSV)

The historian is no more able than any other man to know how often a dying person has transcended this ideology because

he has serenely experienced God's presence in his call. As
surely as God is, in the last analysis, equally present to all eras,
we should expect that it has happened just as it happens today
all around the globe, regardless of the dominant religious and
atheistic ideologies. The question is raised whether God is only
a figment of the imagination or is truly the Lord of our reality.
For the individual, the answer to this question is necessarily
connected with how he answers the question raised by Job, one
confronting us since the conclusion of the preceding chapter. It
has to do with the connection between what one does and what
one experiences, between one's sufferings and God, and,
insofar as one places it in a theoretical context, with the
justification of God, or theodicy, because as the judge of the
whole earth (Gen. 18:25) God should see to it that the good
fortune of a man corresponds to his deserts.[209] The name of the
biblical sufferer, "Job," raises the question symbolically, and in
human as well as creaturely terms: "Where is (my divine)
Father?"[210] Where is the divine Father when it can happen that
a righteous man must suffer in this way?

This is not the place to analyze the literary and theological,
to say nothing of the religio-historical, multilayered composition of the book of Job.[211] In the present connection it must (and
can) suffice if instead of that we take up the central question
which makes up the main part of the book of Job, 3:1–42:6. Job's
friends are held captive by the conviction that there is no
undeserved suffering in this world and that God has punished
every guilty person; hence they are unable to see him as other
than a great sinner. He confronts them with an observation that
evidently runs so sharply contrary to the ideas and beliefs
prevalent in the time of the poet that he has his hero set it forth
only with fearful trembling:

> Look at me, and be appalled,
>   and lay your hand upon your mouth.
> When I think of it I am dismayed,
>   and shuddering seizes my flesh.
> Why do the wicked live,
>   reach old age, and grow mighty in power?
> Their children are established in their presence,

and their offspring before their eyes.
Their houses are safe from fear,
   and no rod of God is upon them.
                                    (21:5-9 RSV)

The declaration that follows about the good fortune of the ungodly gives the impression of the exact opposite of a deuteronomic promise of blessedness (cf Deut. 28:1 ff).[212] The central thrust against the prevailing teaching is provided by the question in statistical terms.

How often is it that the lamp of the wicked is put out?
   That their calamity comes upon them?
   That God distributes pains in his anger?
That they are like straw before the wind,
   and like chaff that the storm carries away?
                                    (21:17-18 RSV)

And at the same time, a new self-consciousness was emerging in opposition to the old dogmatic assumption, which for apologetic purposes was, if possible, being even more rigidly maintained, that there is a connection between one's behavior and the turn of one's fortunes. We cannot understand this new self-consciousness apart from the discussion within Judaism, in which it was coming to terms with its fate of being sent into exile.[213] In the course of that discussion within Judaism, the individual was coming to a consciousness of being responsible for himself. This consciousness came about in view of the over-long and disproportionate impact of the guilt of the fathers, and in view of the dissolution of the old tribal bonds, which occurred at least in part because of the exile and the scattering of people, and by exposure to life in a pagan environment. The later descendants began to utter their taunts:

The fathers used to eat sour grapes,
   and the children's teeth are set on edge as a result!
                                    (Ezek. 18:2)[214]

In response to this, a theologian oriented to the sacral law, probably from the late fourth century B.C., disputed the principle that so closely bound together guilt and punishment: "The soul that sins, it shall die. A son shall not bear the guilt of the father, nor a father the guilt of the son. The righteousness of the righteous shall only come upon him, and the ungodliness of the ungodly shall only come upon him. . . . Therefore, O house of Israel, I shall judge every one of you according to his own conduct, says the Lord Yahweh" (Ezek. 18:20, 30).

We are not assuming that the writer of Job knew this particular writing, but are only suggesting that he fits into discussions such as are also reflected in this book. The friends of Job who are at last unmasked as his adversaries are much more "literary," in accordance with their schooling in "wisdom."[215] The religious responsibility of the individual for the actions of the entire tribe or family has been abandoned by both the author of Ezekiel, with his interest in sacral law, and the poet of the book of Job.

> You say, "God stores up their iniquity for their sons."
>   Let him recompense it to themselves, that they may
>   know it.
> Let their own eyes see their destruction,
>   and let them drink of the wrath of the Almighty.
> For what do they care for their houses after them,
>   when the number of their months is cut off?
>   (Job 21:19-21 RSV)

Thereby one way of solving the problem is cut off, perhaps too radically; perhaps the perspective is too emancipationist, when we consider the realities of a bodily existence that we owe to our parents. But the renunciation of this idea is in keeping with the self-understanding and the sense of what is just and right on the part of the man who also, and particularly, can feel responsible before God only for himself. Then what remains of God's justice?[216] Nothing from which man can derive a rule. What issues from this has a nihilistic sound, and it would indeed be nihilistic if it were not for Job's persistent yearning to be justified by God himself.

> One dies in full prosperity,
>   being wholly at ease and secure,
> his body full of fat
>   and the marrow of his bones moist.
> Another dies in bitterness of soul,
>   never having tasted of good.
> They lie down alike in the dust,
>   and the worms cover them.
>   (21:23-26 RSV)

The positive response of the God who at last appears in the whirlwind turns the tables. Man, who thinks that he can rightly challenge God, in fact is challenged by God;[216] he remains a creature, and as such he is always capable of understanding only a part of the mysteries that are concealed in the creation, although everything is very wisely ordered by God (38 ff). As to its content, the pattern of thought, which is in large measure teleological, is set in opposition to the modern pattern of thought in terms of causes, so consequential in its applications; that is to say, in the former, there is a way of thinking that takes into account the aims and goals involved. Phenomena are not viewed in terms of what has caused them, but in accordance with the characteristic quality of life as a whole, which sustains itself in bodily form as an end in itself, and thus as more than the sum of its causes.[217] God is the Great Teleologist; but if his *tela*, his aims, were subject to man's wholly comprehending them, man would no longer be a creature, but equal to the creator. The explanation of the celestial mystery in the narrative framework of the book of Job remains, in the final analysis, in the train of thought of the poet alone, since Job himself knows nothing of it and in fact cannot know of it. However, it does give to the misery that intrudes without rhyme or reason a meaning that is comprehensible to man, as suffering that bears witness at one and the same time to the dignity of God and of man.[218] And thus in both the material and the answer that is given, the explanation goes beyond the solution provided by the poet, allowing us to disagree over whether this explanation arose so to speak out of academic ruminations or actually out of the quietness of a man who bows before the divine mystery that holds sway in the world. Job 42:6 does not argue unconditionally for the latter solution.

The air becomes thinner and more chill when we turn to the Preacher in Ecclesiastes, the sage who put on the royal mantle, assuming the highest conceivable point of view from which to discuss human possibilities. For him the crucial issue is the question of meaning. And everything that happens under the sun can have meaning only if it does not follow an eternal, aimless circuit (cf Eccles. 1:4 ff), and if man receives back and retains something abiding for all his labors. Like a merchant, the wise man speaks of "profit," and perhaps he thereby gives us a clue as to his actual occupation. What comes of it all? Anyone who does not succeed in gaining something at the very moment has nothing to claim. There is no permanent, abiding profit. And thus he returns again and again to the *carpe diem,* "Seize the day!," which we have already encountered.[219] But even this admonition is not constant. Perhaps he was acquainted, at least by hearsay, with the lot of the slaves of the state who were ruthlessly exploited and crushed in the mines and on the rockpiles.[220] At any rate, the misfortune of the oppressed led him to the view that the deceased are more fortunate than the living, and those who are unborn are more fortunate than either of the others.[221] This view becomes fully comprehensible only against the backgrond of his conviction that a man has to count on everything in his life going against all his wishes and his striving. God has determined the content of the times. And since man does not know what kind of times may await him, his plans are always subject to going awry. Man is like a fish that is caught in a net, or a bird caught in a trap (Eccles. 9:11-12 RSV):

> Again I saw that under the sun the race is not to the swift, nor the battle to the strong, nor bread to the wise, nor riches to the intelligent, nor favor to the men of skill; but time and chance happen to them all. For man does not know his time. Like fish which are taken in an evil net, and like birds which

are caught in a snare, so the sons of men are snared at an evil time, when it suddenly falls upon them.

Thus it is by no means assured that by his good conduct man secures God's favor. Here too God remains the Lord who is beyond our calculations. Thus in the final analysis man can only accept his days as they are given to him, and that means to enjoy the good days and during the evil days to recall that they likewise are made by God (Eccles. 7:13-14; cf 2:24-26).

The probing, piercing observation and inquiry did not make the Preacher happy. Thus he himself conceded, in view of the striving after knowledge:

For in much wisdom is much vexation,
    and he who increases knowledge increases sorrow.
                                    (1:18 RSV)

And in view of the result his confession is as follows: "All this I have tested by wisdom; I said, 'I will be wise';[222] but it was far from me. That which is, is far off, and deep, very deep; who can find it out?" (7:23-24 RSV). His heart obviously has suffered the shock of finitude, so that one is tempted to take his "Everything is vanity" as a transparent film and to read behind it Nietzsche's "For every appetite desires eternity, deep, deep eternity!"

Then who is God, and where is he to be found? We have already indicated that he became an utterly incalculable despot; and one might say that the actual outcome of his rumination is that God encounters man in the fact that, in the present as well as in the future, he himself is ultimately withdrawn. Here God is experienced as the power that sets for man his boundaries that cannot be transcended. And since the Preacher, like the poet of Job, is by nature teleological in his orientation, for him this is willed by God to be thus, so that man may fear God (Eccles. 3:10-15).

It might be said that the poet of Job and the Preacher were attempting to cure their community of an ancient folly. But one must acknowledge a slight doubt as to whether they were successful with their truth. Perhaps one could die more serenely with this truth than with the belief in retribution. The melancholy passages of the book of Ecclesiastes show how difficult it must have been to live with it. The Preacher indeed knew of another possibility, but he did not venture to take it seriously, because it could not be harmonized with his ultimately fatalistic belief. That would have required an altogether different approach. In his view it was sheer presumption for man to regard himself as something better than a beast of the field. In his opinion, one can see how things really are by looking at the seats of judgment, where the person who expects justice falls victim to injustice and, with God's permission, comes to his end like a beast of the field (Eccles. 3:16 ff).[223] In what follows, the Preacher makes a play on the twofold meaning of the word *ruach*, which can mean "breath" as well as "spirit." In verse 19 it is for him the one breath that is common to man and beast. In the question in verse 21, he has in mind the spirit of the deceased. "Who knows, then," he reasons, "whether the spirit of the children of men goes upward and the spirit of the beast goes down to the earth?" In fact, he is thinking of a life after death and wishes to call this possibility into question as nothing but speculation; this is shown by his concluding sentence, which follows the renewed idea of *carpe diem*: "Who can bring him to see what will be after him?" (3:22 RSV).

The skeptical reservations with respect to the solution of the problem of God's justice by means of the expectation of a future life that would bring a settling of accounts could not be maintained for as much as a hundred years in the style of the author of Ecclesiastes. His mode of thought was too skeptical in relation to the tradition of his people to allow that. Jesus ben Sirach, whom we may place in Jerusalem in the first two decades of the second century B.C.,[224] returned to the solution held by the fathers, and therein showed that there cannot be any simple repristination in the course of the history of convictions that have once been called into question; for he reinterpreted the ancient principle with the aid of a Greek idea. In fact death brings the decision, nothing before death, and nothing else but death. He shows how matters are indeed arranged for man. Up to the time of death there is no assurance of salvation for man.[225]

The blessing of the Lord is the reward of the devout,
and he causes his blessing to flourish quickly.
Do not say, "What advantage do I have,
and what will be my prosperity from now on?"
Do not say, "I have enough,
and what evil could befall me from now on?"
In the day of prosperity, no one thinks any more of adversity,
and in the day of adversity, no one thinks any more of
prosperity.
For it is easy in the sight of the Lord, on the day when the
end comes,
to reward a man according to his conduct.
The misfortune of a [single] hour makes one forget his
[former]
luxury,
and at the end of a man's life his deeds will be made
manifest.
Call no one blessed before his death;
a man will be known by his end.

(Ecclus. 11:22-28)[226]

It has rightly been noted that Sirach has appropriated the
crucial concluding idea from Greek tradition; it may remain an
open question whether he became acquainted with it as a
maxim from Solon or from Sophocles.[227] We place it here at the
conclusion in the words of Sophocles, from *Oedipus the King*,
1528 ff.

Therefore wait to see life's ending ere thou count one mortal
blest;
Wait till free from pain and sorrow he has gained his final
rest.

VII. God's Justice and faithfulness— Life out of death

Their bones will rest in the earth, but their spirit will have much joy.

(Jubilees 23:31)

The new ideas of life after death apparently were being discussed in Jerusalem in the time of the teacher whose identity is hidden behind the pseudonym of Koheleth, the preacher or leader of the assembly.[228] In his parrying of these ideas, the preacher summed up his own view in the teaching that was bound to tradition: "Everything goes to one place. Everything came from dust, and everything returns to dust again" (Eccles. 3:20; cf Gen. 3:19).[229]

In another connection we referred to his portrayal of the self-forgetfulness and ultimately the forgottenness of the dead, in order to clarify for us how the Hebrews imagined the deceased souls in the underworld (cf Eccles. 9:4-6).[230] Rendered more cautious by the skepticism of the Preacher, we leaf through his little book once more and note that only in 9:10 does he speak of the underworld, and here presumably in a proverbial utterance. And if in his discourse about the return to the dust, thanks to the correspondence that is characteristically conceived between the stay in the tomb and in Sheol, the thought of the latter could in principle be resonating,[231] still for the Preacher this is questionable. Thus it must be kept seriously in mind that he has dismissed the entire spectral realm of shadows: for him, man goes "to his eternal house," and that means "to his grave" (Eccles. 12:5b).[232] Nothing more can be said about him. As the inscription on a Roman tomb puts it,

"Eternal is this house; here I lie, and here I shall be forever."[233] The view that there is no soul independent of the body, that the very expression itself is meaningless, and that the activities and perceptions of the body are based upon the natural combination of its parts—all this is found in an opinion already noted by the pupil of Aristotle, Dikaiarchos.[234] And Cicero[235] and Lucian[236] give us some intimation of the condescension with which people in the educated circles of the following centuries could look down on the conceptions of the underworld held by the poets and the popular belief.

The Preacher's retreat to ritual observance[237] and a moderation that is dictated by the fear of God represents a reduction. Given the presuppositions of Israel's belief in God's justice that is worked out in the lives of men, such a reduction cannot, in the final analysis, be harmonized with the promises of blessing that are based upon obedience to the Law or with the ardor of belief of the Psalms that struggle with a gracious God. Ultimately the religious persecution, even to the point of martyrdom in the days of the Seleucid Antiochus IV (Epiphanes), posed for every individual the question of what he believed about God's faithfulness and what that faithfulness meant, when there was the possibility that, contrary to all the promises, he might lose his life by being obedient and might save it by being disobedient.[238] In the second century B.C. there was no such thing as *the* answer of Judaism to this question, any more than there had been in the preceding century or was in the following centuries, until after the destruction of the temple and the exclusion of the Sadducees, the Pharisees' belief in the resurrection prevailed.[239]

Thus the question arises whether it is still possible for us to hear the voices of those who, by breaking through the boundary of death that marked the limits of the Preacher's afflictions and thus attributing to him the shadowy realm of the underworld, drew a different conclusion from his observations that God's justice is not unequivocally manifested in this life. The constant testing and sifting of the Old Testament texts in the past two hundred years has led to quite meager results. The great vision in the book of Ezekiel (cf ch 37:1-14) of the reviving of the dry bones is again an example of the imagery that is native to laments and that perceives any and all diminutions of life as seizures by death or the plight of death (cf v 11). For this reason, this passage must be omitted from the list of assured testimonies to the Jewish belief in the resurrection,[240] although it may very well have contributed to keeping the issue alive and to the ultimate prevailing, in Pharisaic circles, of the expectation of the bodily resurrection.[241] This expectation on its own part found the center of its foundation in the belief in God's justice; this is shown by the passage in the Mishna: "All Israel has a share in the world to come, for it is said, 'Thy people consists of pure just ones; they shall forever possess the land' " (cf Isa. 60:21). And the following affirmation shows how central a place this expectation held in the evaluation of belief: "These will have no part in the world to come: he who says that the resurrection of the dead is not found in the Torah (i.e., is not attested in the books of Moses), he who says that the Torah is not from Heaven, and he who denies God."[242]

Many scholars go so far as to recognize only the twelfth chapter of Daniel as an unequivocal witness to the hope of the resurrection in the Old Testament.[243] But this judgment is too restrictive and fails to recognize the intention of the redactional additions in some psalms as well as within the so-called apocalypse of Isaiah (chs 24–27). In the first place we should mention Psalms 49:15 and 73:24 ff. Both of these passages clearly show that the struggle with the problem of the good fortune of the ungodly and the misery of the devout—and that means the problem of the justice of God—has demolished the boundary of death that was traditionally drawn for Old Testament belief. Or perhaps we should, on the authority of Psalm 73, formulate it conversely. Because the reality and the truthfulness of God, and his faithfulness as well, were too firmly assured to be overcome by the vexation of their being incapable of statistical proof and the trouble of one's own sufferings, it was unthinkable that God would allow the bond with his people to be broken in death and thus allow evil in this world to have the last word. Psalm 49 probably originally solved the problem of the good fortune of the ungodly by a two-stage argument, that (1) all men are mortal, and (2) thus even the ungodly rich men must die (cf vv 5-12, 13-14, and 16-20). Thus the psalm appears originally to have remained within the traditional boundaries of the belief in Yahweh. But a later hand has inserted a "new solution" in verse 15.

> But God will ransom my soul (*naphshi*)[244] from the power
>   of the underworld;
> for he will release me.

The key word "release" (*lāqach*) provides the justification in this context for connecting the first clause, not with a deliverance *in the face of*, but *out of*, the underworld.[245] And the case is quite the same in Psalm 73: verses 18-19 suffice to show that here what was originally meant was the end that awaits the ungodly in this world. Then comes verse 24*b*, that with its language does not fit into the original text, and offers the "new solution" from a second hand, "and afterward thou wilt receive me to glory" (RSV). And verse 26 corresponds to this as an expression of a hope that overcomes death.

> My flesh and my heart may fail,
> But God is the strength of my heart and
>   my portion for ever. (RSV)[246]

In both cases, as distinguished from the cases of Enoch and Elijah, what is involved is not a deliverance *from* death, but a deliverance *out of* death. And what here remains related only to the individual is triumphantly extended to the whole of humanity by a similarly later editorial hand in Psalm 22, by including the deceased in the scope of God's lordship.[247]

> For dominion belongs to the Lord,
>   and he rules over the nations.
> Yea, to him shall all the proud of the earth bow down;
>   before him shall bow all who go down to the dust.
> (vv 28-29 RSV)

By means of a contraction of the "Yea, to him" and the change of still another letter, a later hand, which is responsible for the present text, has deleted the great message of the passage. As though the psalm had been connected with its alleged author David, and his death had been seen as a refutation of this interpretation, there follows a further clause: "But his soul has not come to life! Posterity will serve him," and this further serves to confirm the correctness of our reconstruction of the text.

Through the publication of the fragments of an Aramaic manuscript of the book of Enoch, found in Cave Four at Qumran near the Dead Sea, new light has been shed on the age and the development of this composite work.[248] Moreover, it has shed additional light on the history of Jewish eschatology and apocalyptic in general, and upon that of the book of Daniel and of the passages from the psalms just cited in particular. While in these psalms the circumstances of the deliverance from the underworld remain obscure, even the prophecy in the last chapter of the book of Daniel provides more of allusions to these particulars than disclosures of them. Apparently the authors of these texts could presuppose that their contemporaries, or at least a narrower circle of those being addressed, possessed the more specific information, so that they could content themselves with these allusions. In seeking to unlock the meaning of these passages, the present-day reader can be entirely too quick to seek here the familiar physical, bodily resurrection, which presumably is in fact attested in Ezekiel 37:13b-14 and Isaiah 26:19;[249] the inclination may be to see it here in the form of a wholly new creation such as is first clearly attested in 2 Maccabees 7:28-29 (cf v 11).[250] He should be warned against this mistake by Psalm 49:15, since with the deliverance from the underworld he obviously thinks of the liberation of the soul of the deceased from the sleep of death. But this conception may not be assumed with certainty to be found in Jesus or even in Paul; a glance at Mark 12:25[251] and at 1 Corinthians 15:50 (cf vv 35 ff [252]) will suffice to show this. If striking correspondences between the texts cited—and among them particularly the last chapter of Daniel, written in 166 or 165 B.C.—and the eschatological conceptions of the still earlier "Book of the Watchmen" (Enoch 1–36) should appear, we would be justified in interpreting the obscurities from the perspective of the earlier—and in the case of the additions to the psalms, perhaps contemporary—book of Enoch.

Daniel 12:1-3 (RSV) reads as follows:

> 1. At that time shall arise Michael, the great prince who has charge of your people. And there shall be a time of trouble, such as never has been since there was a nation[253] till that time; but at that time your people shall be delivered, every one whose name shall be found written in the book. 2. And many of those who sleep in the dust of the earth shall awake, some to everlasting life, and some to shame and everlasting contempt. 3. And those who are wise shall shine like the brightness of the firmament; and those who turn many to righteousness, like the stars for ever and ever."

Here there is opened up to the initiated a section out of the eschatological drama that spans nations and cosmos, that according to the conviction of the apocalyptist was already in full course and would reach its climax and conclusion in the very near future (cf 11:40 and 12:11-12). Zion would stand in the very center of the final confrontation between the God of Israel and the world powers (cf 10:20-21; 11:45). In this struggle, Michael, one of the seven archangels known to us from Enoch 20:1 ff,[254] intervenes to deliver God's people. Yet the reference to those who are written in the celestial book shows that in this connection there will be a great separation, and thus a great judgment will be involved (cf Enoch 98:7-8).[255] And so, just as from among the living only a part will be saved, so also there will be a separation among the many who are raised: some to eternal life, and we can complete the parallel without hesitation; over against these stand the ungodly and apostates. In this connection the key word "contempt" points back to Isaiah 66:24, where there is the warning that in the time of salvation, pilgrims to Jerusalem will go out to the gates of the city to look at the bodies of the sinners that burn there and are eaten by worms forever, to the abhorrence of all mankind. On the other hand, there is a promise to "those who are wise" of a brilliant existence that will be their abiding characteristic. According to 11:33 ff, these are the spiritual leaders of the anti–hellenistic

resistance, and among them, in keeping with the perspective of
the book of Daniel, presumably in particular the apocalyptists,
the teachers of the eschatological secrets of history. These,
through their testimony, serve to hold steadfast those who
waver in their faithfulness toward the Law and the faith of their
fathers.[256] It is not said how the resurrection comes about and
why only "many" (not all) will arise. This does not necessarily
refer to the deceased who rest in their tombs, in the land
covered with dust; this is evident from the occasional
connection of the "dust" with the underworld.[257] Certainly it
should not be overlooked that the thrust of concern in the
eschatological instruction is the interest of the contemporaries;
the disclosure of the destiny of those faithful to the Law as well
as of the apostates is intended to help the former to endure the
distresses of the present time without being led astray from
their belief in the power of Yahweh. But it could nevertheless
be premature to draw from this perspective the conclusion that
when he speaks of the "many" the apocalyptist is thinking solely
of the deceased and still surviving contemporaries of the
religious struggles since the middle of the seventies in
Jerusalem.[258]

Now let us turn to the eschatology of the "Book of the
Watchmen" in the book of Enoch, as it is revealed in the course
of the exploration of the entire cosmos by the patriarch after he
was taken up; this is found particularly in chapters 22 and
24–27. On his cosmic journey, Enoch himself purportedly
relates in chapter 22,[259] how he comes to a great mountain in the
distant West that contains the chambers of the spirits of the
deceased, in which they are preserved until the great day of
judgment (22:3-4). Although the passage first speaks of four
caves or chambers, three of them dark and the fourth illumined
and provided with a spring (v 2), later it speaks of only three
such chambers. One of them is for those who already, in their
lifetime, are judged, the utterly ungodly sinners. Since their
punishment has already befallen them, they will not come out
of their caves and thus will not have a share in the resurrection
(cf 22:13). Another cave, dark like the first one, is for the sinners
who are not punished during their lifetime, who on the great
day of judgment are condemned to eternal torment (vv 10-11).

And finally, there is the section illumined by a source of radiance, for the spirits of the righteous (22:9). Here we rightly are reminded of the petition of Dives to Father Abraham, in the parable of Dives and Lazarus (Luke 16:24) and thus are made aware that people were already on the way to attributing life to the souls of the deceased in the intermediate state. In the fourth section, of which we had a glimpse at the outset, it appears that we are dealing with a chamber for those who are stricken in innocence, and thus for the martyrs, of whom the spirit of Abel is a prototype (cf Rev. 6:9-10; Heb. 11:4). In surveying the entire portrayal, one can hardly escape the conclusion that here an earlier three-chamber schema, which had a division into special places for the good, the in-between group, and the wicked, has been adapted to the author's own way of thinking. The latter, on the one hand, in accordance with the traditional sharp separation between the devout and the ungodly, had no use for the middle group, about whom judgment would have to be rendered only later. On the other hand, this way of thinking had to take into account the problem of the good fortune of the ungodly and the innocent suffering and death of the righteous.

Before we look for the possible stimuli responsible for this conception of the underworld, we must pursue the eschatological expectations of the book as far as is appropriate to the context of our subject. The vexing question in the interpretation of chapters 22 and 24–27 actually consists in the fact that it is not quite clear what becomes of the souls of the righteous in their lighted cave, whether they remain in it or return to the light of day. Later on it is promised to the righteous and those who are meek that they will eat of the tree that has been transplanted from God's garden to Jerusalem and will live longer than the patriarchs; and that means at least a thousand years (cf Gen. 5:20), but by no means eternally (Enoch 25:4 ff). Since there is a reluctance to have the righteous dead suffer death again,[260] it is possible that here the narrator, who is concerned with the fate of those who will be living at the time of the final judgment and of the ungodly ones who have died, has passed over something, perhaps because in this passage he was governed by the text he had already before him.[261] Since he had such strong views, altogether in accord with Isaiah 66:24, of the fate of the condemned who would be cast into the accursed ditch outside the gates of Jerusalem (Enoch 27), we should credit him also with having well-established views of the future of the righteous dead. In my opinion the puzzle is solved by the book of Jubilees, chapter 23. This book, written in the last decades of the second century B.C., recasts the book of Genesis according to the taste of the times, so that is has even been called the "little Genesis."[262] In it, in connection with a great persecution, the Israelites are credited with a new obedience to the Law, which has as its consequence a lifespan that increases to a thousand years (Jub. 23:26 ff).[263] While this new generation rises up at last and drives out its foes (23:30), the righteous look on with gratitude and rejoice for all eternity in the judgment upon their enemies. Now the following verse (31) shows that these righteous ones spoken of here are the spirits of the righteous who are deceased; for this verse says: "And their bones will rest in the earth, and their spirits will have great joy, and they will recognize that it is God who exercises judgment and shows mercy to hundreds and thousands and (indeed) to all those who love him" (cf Exod. 20:5-6). Or, to put it in another way: on the great judgment day, the spirits of the righteous are set free from their chamber in order now to live again eternally as spirits. And the author of the book of Enoch, which is only slightly later, similarly explains (Enoch 91–105)[264] that the spirits of the righteous will not pass away (103:4), but will shine like the stars of heaven, and the gates of heaven will be opened to them where, like the angels, they will have great joy (Enoch 104:2, 4). What was it that Jesus said to the Sadducees? "When they rise from the dead, they will neither marry nor be given in marriage, but they are like the angels in heaven" (Mark 12:25).

If we look back now at Daniel 12:1-3, its riddles are suddenly resolved: because the wicked who are already judged remain in their chamber, it is not all that are raised, but only "many."[265] These "many" are, on the one hand, the spirits of the ungodly who during their lifetime were spared the punishment that they deserved and are destined for eternal damnation, and, on the other hand, the spirits of the righteous that are destined for eternal life. Among these, only the teachers receive the glorified light-figure. But according to what has already been said, there is hardly any doubt that they all receive their new and permanent home in heaven (cf Phil. 3:10). One of the readers of the Isaiah-apocalypse has later inserted in 25:8 the words, "He shall destroy death for ever."[266] With these words, if our judgment is correct, he has sought succinctly to summarize the hopes whose emergence we have traced out here.

In the *descensus ad inferos,* which was perhaps first appended to the Acts of Pilate at the point where we pass from antiquity to the Middle Ages, the Crucified One after his death invades Hades, which thereby is illumined even to its most remote corner. Then with his right hand he grasps the patriarch Adam, stands him upright, and addresses all the deceased. "Come to me, all you who were put to death by the cross which this one has touched. For behold! I raise all of you by means of the wood of the cross. Then he brought them all forth. . . . As he was going forth, there followed him the holy fathers and lifted their song of praise: Blessed be he who comes in the name of the Lord! Alleluia! He is deserving of honor and praise from all the saints."[267] And with this we understand what the church means with the statement *descendit ad infera,* "he descended into the realm of the dead."

VIII. Epilogue:
Roots and directions

Now of course it is not fitting for a thoughtful person to insist that what I have said is just this way. But that this or something like it is true concerning our souls and their abodes—since the soul is immortal, one may properly hold this with firmness, for it is worthy of the venture of belief. It is a splendid venture, and one should recite such things as if they were a magical charm. This is why I have dwelt so long in delivering my story.

(Plato, *Phaedo,* 114D)

We could have concluded our study with the insights gained in the last chapter and let it go at that. With those insights, after all, we had come full circle to the expectations of the Wisdom of Solomon that engaged our attention at the outset, since our entire treatment has been, as it were, a historical commentary on his assurance and confidence that the souls of the righteous are in God's hands, free from torment (3:1).[268] But how is this expectation, which can be demonstrated as present since the third century B.C. and which finally deserves the name of the hope of immortality, related to the testimony of the belief of the Persians and the Greeks who shaped its beginnings? This question arises on its own initiative in the study of Enoch 22. Therefore it is obligatory upon us to explore it, at least as an appendix, with the caution that is required in this extremely difficult field and with the brevity required in the present context.

For more than two hundred years the Persians were the rulers of the Jews. It is impossible to assume that there would have been no direct or indirect contact with their way of thinking during this time.[269] When we seek to determine what, after all, the Persians could have contributed to the Jews in the area of expectations of the hereafter, we are confronted with the difficulties that mount up before anyone who wishes to concern himself with the sacred writings of the Zoroastrians and Parsees, the so-called Avesta, which arose in an apparently very complicated and by no means clear process of tradition.[270] Therefore it is possible only with great hesitation to attribute a particular idea to the persian priest-prophet Zarathustra, or at least to the pre-Sassanid era. The scholars themselves are not in agreement whether the founder of this religion lived around 1000 B.C. or not until about 600 B.C. This fact in itself sheds some light on the nature and quality of the data available to us.[271] But even the escape device of retreating altogether to the historically datable pronouncements of Greek authors is not without its own set of problems; in using them, one must weigh the actual source-value that they possess after one has subtracted all the tendentious elements and has taken into account any possible misunderstandings.[272]

On the other hand, just as there was in Asia Minor a Hellenism already a hundred years before Alexander,[273] we may assume similarly for Palestine a certain Greek cultural influence, corresponding to the economic and political activities of the Greeks in the eastern Mediterranean basin especially in the fifth and fourth centuries B.C., before the conquest of Palestine by the Macedonian.[274] The conditions in Jerusalem in the first third of the second century B.C. give sufficient information about the vigor of this influence in the hellenistic era.[275] The problem of the borrowings of religious ideas is well known. Such borrowing may range all the way from the communication of thoughts by means of the written word, to hearsay, and even to the word that—torn out of its context, thrown out, and picked up—sets in motion in its hearer a movement of his own. Anyone who keeps in mind this problem will assume a stance of caution from the very outset. If one leaves out of consideration the upper level of Judaism in the Persian court, for example (cf Neh. 1–2), and later in Jerusalem, in accordance with the basic religious conviction that was native to Judaism, one will hardly be able to assume a conscious curiosity with reference to strange, alien beliefs. For the same reason, it may very well have appeared only rarely even in the leading circles. If we call to mind moreover the fact that in any case we have preserved for us from the Zoroastrian literature only fragments and from the Greek-hellenistic literature only selections, our expectations of being able to adduce compelling proof of some foreign influences are still further reduced.

If we wish to avoid the discussions of the specialists in Iranian religion over the question whether Zarathustra held an actual belief in the resurrection or only something preliminary to such belief,[276] one will, more in keeping with the aim of our reflections, hold to a summary of the expectations that presumably can be assumed for Zarathustra's followers between the sixth century B.C. and the third century A.D.: When a man has died, his soul must appear before its judges and then must walk across the infinitely narrow bridge of decision, the famous *cinvato peretu*. The good survive the danger and unscathed attain the realm of light, while the evil plunge into the abyss of Ahriman, the spirit of falsehood. At the end of the last of the three-times-three-thousand-year periods, which are filled with the struggle between the wise lord, Ahura Mazda, and Ahriman, the dead will rise and walk through a stream of molten metal; in this ordeal the righteous will feel no pain at all, the wicked will be purged, and Ahriman together with all the evil powers will be destroyed forever.[277] A note preserved in Plutarch, dating back to the historian Theopompos of Chios in the fourth century B.C., adds to the picture by saying that those who are resurrected require no food and cast no shadows.[278] Thus it appears that a transfigured corporeality was ascribed to them. We note as a distinctive feature that the Iranians anticipated a judgment of the dead that would take place immediately after death and a purification of the dead that would occur at the end of the world-epoch.

If we consider the diversity of Greek intellectual life that is manifested in poetry, philosophy, and the mystery religions, it is clear that any attempt within our present context to provide a general overview of the post-Homeric developments in beliefs about the dead would be doomed to failure. Moreover, it would quickly become evident that there is just as much disagreement over what is to be labeled Orphic, Pythagorean, Eleusinian, and Platonic as over the mysteries and secrets of the Avesta. One may however regard it as assured that in the Eleusinian mystery religion a distinction was made between the destiny after death of the initiated person and that of the person who had not been initiated.[279] And it may likewise be regarded as probable that the idea that after death the souls become stars goes back to Pythagoreanism.[280] The sea of stars in the Milky Way must have played a special role in this connection, though being no more than a transitional stage for the souls in the cycle of their births. Among the Orphics, who regarded the body as the prison of the soul, the punishments of the underworld apparently played a special role along with the idea of the migration of the soul.[281] It appears certain that Plato made distinctive and arbitrary use of all these materials in the shaping of his myths.[282] Thus in the work of his old age, the *Timaeus*, he has the souls of those who have led a perfect life released from the cycle of births and brought to the stars as their home.[283] In

Phaedo he had Socrates declare that in connection with the judgment, the dead were assigned to a place of abode corresponding to their lives; those who belonged to an in-between category would be sent into the deep blue Stygian Sea as a place of purification, while the evildoers would be dragged into Tartarus, not to escape from thence until they were forgiven by the ones whom they had injured in their lifetime. But those who had understood their life on this earth as a probation, having escaped the necessity of being placed in a body once again, would return to the lofty heights of the true earth.[284] To the extent that in antiquity the insight into the spherical shape of the earth prevailed, there was no room left for Homer's underworld and the blessed islands of the distant West. Thus also the growing astronomical insight led to the placing of the realms of the hereafter, the underworld and the region of the blessed, in the realm of the stars.[285] For the ideas of faith can retain their transcendental content only if they take into account the current knowledge of the world. And perhaps not least of all this is the basis for the attraction that the ancient idea of reincarnation is able to exert for the present day.

Only our concluding reflections have some reference to possible dependence of Jewish eschatology upon the ideas and beliefs of its environment. If we look back at the Jewish expectations, we see a clear difference between the Zoroastrian and the Greek belief about the judgment of the dead and the Jewish belief about a final judgment. In this connection, Enoch 22 remains indefinite as to what basis governs the assignment of the souls of the dead to their various chambers.[286] In any case, one can conjecture that in the apocalyptist's celestial world that was populated by angelic beings there were angels who would convey the dead to the place that would be in harmony with the life they had lived. The stimulus leading to acceptance of the idea of an underworld divided into three parts could, if the apocalyptist of Enoch 22 had not reworked an earlier Jewish source that is unknown to us, go back to Greek influence; and here perhaps it is an Orphic description of the underworld, a Nekyia, and the direct or indirect encounter with such a teaching of itinerant Orphic preachers sufficed to provide that stimulus.[287]

The belief that the ones who have achieved their consummation receive a glorified light-form and a heavenly home could be mediated from the East or from the West, to whatever extent it was not fed altogether from the sources of a popular faith that is not otherwise attested. The belief that at the end of time the spirits of the dead will awaken is a Jewish solution that is connected with the expectation of a final judgment. The East could have prompted the thought that they will be raised. The open question, which is posed for the historian of religion in light of the further development since the close of the sixth century B.C., in Greek belief about the hereafter, also arises again in view of the conquest of the boundary of death by Israel's faith. What significance attaches to Iranian religion as the direct or indirect stimulus to the enlivening of this hope? Of course, stimuli are received and made effective only when the recipient is ripe for them, and the solutions that are offered are in the last analysis compatible with the recipient's own perspective. In this sense, the Jewish idea of the resurrection was indebted to its own roots, its own heritage.

B.
DEATH AND LIFE
IN THE
NEW TESTAMENT

I. The power of death

a) Death as inescapable fate

Every human being is moving inexorably toward the hour of his death that strikes for him at the end of his life's journey. There is no escape from this destiny. This bitter awareness was only all too clearly felt by the people of the ancient world. "It is appointed unto man once to die" (Heb. 9:27). Every man must bow to this recognition, no matter how gladly he would close his eyes to it or escape its force. Ultimately all men must suffer death. Rebellion against this harsh truth, quiet resignation, muted grief, or indulgent enjoyment of every day that is granted to one—in all these ways of conduct there is the assertion of the awareness that everything has its time, and no one, nothing, can elude the end which is death.[288]

Perplexity and confusion that people experienced in the face of the death of others close to them are reflected in the burial inscriptions that were dedicated to the deceased. Such messages as "May the dust rest lightly upon you" or "In everlasting remembrance" were inscribed there, and the wish was expressed that the departed might rest in peace. One might be seized by his fate today, and another not until tomorrow, but no one would elude it entirely. Hence all men must look toward the day which will sooner or later be the last one.[289] From the second century A.D. there is preserved a letter of consolation written by an Egyptian woman to parents who had lost their son. In it she says that she grieves with them as she once had wept over the loss of "the blessed one," her husband or perhaps her son. And then she continues: "But of course there is no recourse with something like this. So comfort each other."[290] Words fail the writer of the letter in her perplexity. Overcome by distress, she falls silent and offers a comfort that is after all no comfort; no one can do anything against the inexorable fate.

Anyone who knows what death is has also grasped the meaning of life. The Greek historian Herodotus tells that in ancient Egypt it was a custom during a banquet to carry about a wooden figure resembling a corpse in a coffin and to show it to all the participants in the feast. They were supposed to look upon the representation of death in their eating and drinking to be conscious of the fact that sometime every one of them would die (Herodotus II.78). Only the person who thinks about death and is fully aware that his days must come to an end will also know how rightly to enjoy the pleasures of life. It was Herodotus' intention that by his use of this narrative the Greeks would be prompted to hold to this example themselves.

Educated men remembered the exemplary conduct of Socrates, who in the face of approaching death talked with his disciples, with unruffled calm, about death and decay, life and immortality. Plato, in his dialogue *Phaedo*, portrays Socrates' end and praises him by saying that "of his contemporaries whom we have known, he was, we may say, the very best and most insightful and most upright of all" (118A). He did not fall into mournful lamentations, but accepted the fate that was imposed upon him with dignified calm; he was sustained by the conviction that God and the Idea of life itself, and whatever else is immortal, would never perish. "When death comes to a man, then what is mortal about him, it appears, dies, but what is immortal and imperishable withdraws from death and goes its way intact" (106E). From this expectation arose the hope that the soul of man might be immortal, might be released from the perishable body at the moment of death, and might ascend to celestial bliss (64C). Death is inflicted upon man as a natural occurrence to which all creation alike is subjected. But not until death does man attain his goal, because now the soul enters into the immortality for which it is destined. This conviction lives in man as a strong hope (114CD). It fills him and sustains him through the difficult hours of dying. If he believes in the immortality of the soul, he will not fear death. He will rather so mold his life that the soul pursues its true destiny and guides his deeds and activities down to the last moment. This philosophical teaching was widespread in the ancient world and afforded comfort to many people.

Yet these ideas were contradicted, because they could not be compellingly demonstrated and therefore had to remain the expression of an uncertain expectation. No messenger had ever come back from the other world to report on conditions and events there. In the teaching of the philosopher Epicurus it was said that in death the human body is dissolved into its component parts and disintegrates, without any of it continuing to maintain its existence. But since anything that is dissolved no longer has any feeling, in the final analysis death does not affect us. For anything that has no feeling, no sensitivity, has no meaning for us (Diogenes Laertius X.139). Thus there remained the sober and helpless declaration that there is nothing we can do against death; we have no recourse. Grief, lamentation, and weeping seize those who are left behind, who have been deprived of a kinsman or friend. They strive to overcome the distress by submitting to the dispensations of providence and acknowledging its incomprehensible wisdom.[291]

The Stoic philosophy therefore urged people inwardly to detach themselves early from life and its goods, in order then to be able to bid them farewell unburdened. The philosopher Epictetus sums up this idea in a graphic figure.

> If during a voyage, when the ship is lying in port, you go ashore to get water, you may incidentally pick up a shellfish or a mushroom along the way. But your thoughts must be turned toward the ship. You must constantly look back, to see whether the captain is calling you. And when he calls, you must leave all those things, so that you may not have to be carried on board, tied up like a sheep. So is it also in life. If instead of little mushrooms or shellfish you are granted a wife or a child, there is no objection to that. But if that captain calls, hurry to the ship, leaving all these things behind and never looking back. But if you are an old man, never go far from the ship, lest you be left behind when he calls. (*Enchiridion* 7)

Anyone who is able to enjoy everything modestly and moderately, and to keep in mind that nothing is given to him as a permanent possession, will be able to practice the art of being mindful always of death as the end of all things, and intelligently to manage the days that are given to him.

b) Death as judgment

In devout circles of the Judaism of late antiquity, people strove to find an explanation for the fate of death by reflecting upon the culpable conduct of Adam and considering its consequences. Thus they traced the origin of death back to the fact that, although God had indeed created man for eternal life, through the devil's jealousy death had come into the world (Wis. of Sol. 2:23-24). The devil led the first men astray, to disobey God's commandment, and thereby opened the door to the fate of death. In various writings that treat of the approaching end of this world and the dawning of God's new world, there appears the question why this world is inexorably hastening toward destruction.[292] The answer that is given is that this calamitous destiny had its beginning already with Adam. God had imposed upon him one single commandment—namely, that he should not eat of the one forbidden fruit (Gen. 2:16-17; 3:1-7)—but he had disregarded this commandment. The punishment for this disobedience as God's judgment followed close on its heels, for God then pronounced death upon him and all his descendants (4 Ezra 3:7). "Because of his evil heart the first Adam fell into sin and guilt, and likewise all those who are born of him" (4 Ezra 3:21-22). Thus the cry of lamentation: "O Adam, what have you done! When you sinned, your fall came not only upon you, but also upon us, your descendants" (4 Ezra 7:118). Consequently Adam brought death into the world and shortened the lifespan of those who were descended from him (Syr. Bar. 17:3). Thereby an explanation was offered that was supposed to identify the origin of the fate of death. Yet it still remained an enigma why not only Adam had to die, but along with him all men were subjected to the same fate. An attempt to find a solution was made with the following reflection: "If Adam first sinned and brought premature death upon all, yet every single one of those who are descended from him has brought upon himself the future pain, and again every single one of them has chosen the future glory. . . . Thus Adam is solely and exclusively responsible for himself, and every one of us has become Adam for himself" (Syr. Bar. 54:15, 19).[293] The Jewish scribes attempted to illumine the obscure connection between the fate of death and man's sinful guilt by formulating the concise maxim, "There is no death without sin and no suffering without guilt."[294] Nevertheless they did not succeed in finding a solution to the contradiction-laden problem. For on the one hand, it was said that through Adam's disobedience death was brought upon all mankind. But on the other hand, it was not asserted that Adam's bad example had had the effect of bringing upon all his descendants a compulsion to sin. Death is inescapable for all men, but the evil deed is not inescapable. Herewith is posed the problem of how sin and death, guilt and destiny, are related.

c) Death in the world

The apostle Paul, whose epistles are the earliest literary documents in the cluster of New Testament writings, takes up these reflections and continues them in the fifth chapter of his Epistle to the Romans.[295] In order to indicate the universal scope of the salvation that was wrought by Christ, he compares it with the ruin that had once begun with Adam's deed and since then had rested as a burden of fate upon all men. In this context, it is not the question of the power of death that forms the point of departure for his train of thought, but rather conversely, Paul argues from the immeasurable greatness of the salvation and sets in contrast to it the opposing picture of humanity represented by Adam. Because the light that has come into the world with Christ illumines the darkness, the previously hidden features come to light more clearly than heretofore. Hence, Paul first describes the dominion that sin and death had gained over the whole of humanity from Adam onward (Rom. 5:12-14). Then he attaches a further step in his train of thought, in which he shows the difference between Adam and Christ. It is true that the one, like the other, has set in motion an occurrence that thenceforward affected the whole of mankind.

But the events and effects that issued from them were utterly different. For righteousness and life, which began with Christ, have an infinitely wider range than sin and death, which found their entrance into the world through Adam (Rom. 5:15-17). With this limitation, which to be sure is crucial, the contrast between Adam and Christ then is carried farther, by setting in opposition the fate that once came upon all men and the life and righteousness that now have come with Christ (Rom. 5:18-19). The last two sentences of the paragraph round off the train of thought and praise the incomprehensible superabundance of the grace that triumphs over sin, law, and death (5:20-21).

Death came into the world through Adam's deed (1 Cor. 15:21)—Paul presupposes this principle, which Jewish doctrine had formulated, and he agrees with it. But he also carries this utterance farther, by significantly deepening it in light of the message of Christ. The ideas follow so closely one upon the other that the sentence structure breaks down and remains incomplete: "As then sin entered into the world through a man, and death by sin, and thus death came to all men, because all have sinned"—Paul is not able to pull together these utterances, with all their excessive weight; instead, he starts off again, to describe the universal dominion of death with the aid of further reflection.

What happened at the beginning? For Paul, at the beginning stands the figure of Adam. He was the man who came from the hand of the Creator, and therefore is to be regarded as the representative of all men. In this connection Paul speaks in an extremely dense, close-knit argument. In his introductory sentence he mentions only the one man, without speaking of his conduct or his disobedience. Only later, in verses 18-19, does he come to speak of these. It is sufficient only to refer to Adam in order to be aware at once of what happened in his story. Here Paul speaks first of sin and then subsequently mentions death. Only rarely does he speak about sins, understood as transgressions of God's commandments—generally his customary way of speaking. Instead, he sharpens the focus of the concept of sin, by speaking of it consistently in the singular and in understanding it as the power that from Adam onward has established its compelling dominion over all men. All are subject to it, and no one is able to escape it.

However, this power did not come alone; with it, death too came into the world. With this statement Paul takes up the apocalyptic conceptions of the origins of the fate of death, but at the same time he significantly goes beyond those conceptions. For first of all he speaks of sin and of its irrestistible dominion over the world. If this fate that is imposed upon all men must be characterized as inescapable, still sin also occurs in the culpable actions of every individual man. For this reason the apostle adds, "because all have sinned." Thus, what happened in Adam's disobedience is repeatedly done again in the disobedience of every individual man. On the one hand, he finds himself always in a predetermined situation that bears the marks of fate. But on the other hand, he senses that through his own conduct he is constantly in opposition to God's commandment and guidance. No one is able to free himself from this vicious circle of fate and guilt. The proof of this is provided by the destiny of death that looms over all men without exception. Someone indeed might object that after all sin can be identified only when there is a written law by which it can be measured. But even before Israel had received the Law at Sinai, sin was already powerfully at work in all the world as a ruling force (Rom. 5:13). For all Adam's descendants were under the effects of his transgression, from which they were unable to detach themselves (v 14).

Nowhere in Judaism had anyone spoken in such radical terms of sin and the fate of death that is bound up with it. Some asserted that there are among men some righteous persons who actually have kept God's commandments and thus have demonstrated that there is no universal enslavement to sin. They believed that the ascension of Moses or that of Elijah proved that these devout men of Israel had escaped death and had been taken up directly into the celestial world. But Paul knows no exceptions. All men are subject to sin and death. It is not Paul's intention with this affirmation to give expression to a thoroughly pessimistic world view. He does not intend to speak of the nature of man in profound skepticism. But he is thinking from the perspective of the cross of Christ, and he recognizes that the power of sin and death has enslaved all men, so that no one is able to liberate himself from this captivity. In this context sin and death had made use of the aid of the Law, in order to make their dominion simply irresistible. But "God has sent his Son in the form of flesh that is subject to sin and for sin, and has condemned sin in the flesh" (Rom. 8:3). This means that Christ became man and thereby entered into the realm of the dominion of sin and death. Nevertheless he remained obedient to God, and did not become disobedient like Adam and all his descendants. Thus he went his way to death, which he suffered on the cross (Phil. 2:8), thereby defeating sin on its own grounds. "It was a strange conflict, when life and death contended; Life gained the victory, and swallowed up death. The Scripture has proclaimed how one death destroyed the other, and death itself has become a mockery." Thus sings Martin Luther in his Easter hymn, exactly striking the note of Pauline thought.

Through his death Christ conquered death, which ever since Adam has exercised its irresistible rule in the world. Therefore it is only from the perspective of the cross of Christ that it becomes manifest what sin and death in reality are. In this connection Paul is not thinking that sin is passed on from one generation to the next like an evil inheritance, in a biological sense. But sin is enmity against God (Rom. 8:7), in which man always finds himself. But this enmity is also man's guilt, with which he rebels against God. Death comes as the fitting wages for this rebellion (Rom. 6:23). In this context the meaning of death is not limited to the physical demise to which all living beings are subject. Instead, the term also denotes alienation from God, in which all of man's thinking and doing, life and work, in the final analysis fall victim to nothingness.

The fact that all men must die is not to be understood simply as a natural end that no creature can escape. Death cannot be detached from its connection with human guilt. Because man wants to live without God and arbitrarily to gain and to mold the meaning of his life from his own resources, and because he rebels against God or even denies him, man becomes subject to judgment and must die. Hence, it is precisely in death that the guilt of men becomes manifest, the guilt by which they are separated from God.[296]

But Adam is a "type of the one to come" (v 14). In this language Paul calls the first man a counterpart of the last man, but more: he no longer sees mankind in terms of the omen of Adam and of the human fate that he set in motion. Instead, he looks at the world from the perspective of the cross of Christ; the world now stands under the sign of the lordship of Christ. Christ therefore is the central figure, the type, and Adam is the antitype. As Adam once through his conduct also determined the destiny of all men, so now through Christ something has happened that affects the whole world.

In the Judaism of that time there was often thoughtful reflection concerning the fateful figure of the first man. And in the philosophical and religious reflections of the hellenistic world, there were many ideas offered concerning the appearance of a primal man who stood at the beginning of all human life. But at the end a heavenly redeemer would appear, who would liberate enslaved mankind. Yet in all these diverse concepts there was no immediate prototype that Paul could simply have taken over. Instead, he exercises great freedom in making use of first one conception and then another available to him, adapting them to fit the needs of his line of argument. Thus, for example, he appropriated the apocalyptic statements that have to do with the circumstances of death brought about by Adam and fitted them into his own pattern of thought. In so doing he significantly altered these statements, because he now uses them to expound and explicate the message of Christ.[297] In the light of that message there is opened up to him an entirely new understanding of the story of Adam and the history of all his descendants. As through Adam death came into the world, so through Christ life came. This means that through the death of Jesus Christ, death is deprived of its power, and indeed is slain. For because the dominion of sin is broken, death has lost its sting by which it oppressed and enslaved men.[298]

Only because he knows of the power of the Resurrection and of life, which had its inception with Christ, can Paul speak with such sharpness of the power of death that holds sway in the world. Christ and Adam can be compared with each other, because the one, like the other, has set in motion an event that has changed the world and placed a definitive mark upon it; but in this very comparison at the same time an essential difference becomes manifest, which must make the comparison appear inadequate. Therefore the apostle sets limits upon the placing of Adam and Christ over against each other, by stating in verses 15-17 that in the final analysis the two cannot be compared. Even though the ruin that Adam caused provides the background against which the worldwide significance of Christ's saving act is set forth, it must now be said that the latter far surpasses the former. Therefore in the final analysis Adam's sinful act does not correspond to Christ's act of grace (v 15). The gift of salvation cannot simply be compared with the effects that issued from the act of sin (v 16). And the fate of death, which was brought on by the one Adam, cannot ultimately be compared with the life and righteousness that have come to reign through the one Jesus Christ (v 17). Only by the use of an intensifying "so much the more" can the comparison be maintained.

Through the transgression of the one man it has come about that all must die. But the demonstration of God's grace and the gift of grace of the one man Jesus Christ are only the more richly applied to all. Through the act of disobedience of the one man, death achieved its dominion. But all the more surely, through the one Jesus Christ, all those who have received the fullness of grace and the gift of justification will gain the victory. Set in contrast to the reign of death, to which all men are subject in consequence of Adam's deed, is the far more comprehensive reign of grace and life which had its beginning with Christ. Here the passage speaks, on the one hand, of the dominion of death. But on the other hand, the dominion or supremacy of grace is understood in personal terms. For it is said that those who belong to Christ will reign with him. It is not only in some distant future, in which the coming world will take the place of this world that is characterized by sin and death, but now, already, that the kingdom of grace is established. The judgment that is pronounced upon the life of man is no longer that of nothingness, but of righteousness. Of course, this effect does not occur by compulsion, as did the consequence of Adam's deed, which came as fatal corruption upon all men. But the gift of grace seeks to be accepted: righteousness needs to be received in faith. In this way the step is taken from Adam's side to Christ's side, in order to pass from death to life. The ultimate decision hinges upon this alternative, Adam or Christ. No one can continue to evade the choice. For no one now stands at the beginning in such a way that the choice is not already placed before him. Hence the whole world is now defined by this alternative, and in the life of every individual person the issue between the two options must be argued out and decided.[299]

After Paul has sketched this alternative, he can bring this train of thought to its conclusion. If sin has brought in death and with the help of the Law established its compulsory dominion over all the world, so all the more must grace, by virtue of justification unto eternal life, reign through Jesus Christ our Lord (v 21). Therewith the apostle once more emphasizes that he views death in the light of the life, and nothingness from the perspective of the righteousness, which has come into the world through Christ. He does not deny that every man still remains subject to physical death and must die. Nevertheless, he stoutly denies that this death still may be understood as lostness and alienation from God. Instead, both death and life are to be seen in the context of belonging to the crucified and resurrected Christ. Christ has established his lordship over all the world and intends to include in that lordship and reign all those who belong to him. The apostle wants to emphasize the incomparable glory and splendor of life and its utterly victorious power, and therefore he measures it against the greatest power that had existed in the world up to that time, the power of sin and death. Yet even these powers pale into insignificance in comparison with the overwhelming greatness of the gift of grace that God has bestowed upon the world in Christ. Therewith Paul clearly indicates that in his reflections on death and life, Adam and Christ, he is expounding the primitive Christian confession of the crucified and risen Lord and is portraying the consequences that are to be drawn therefrom for the Christians' believing, loving, and hoping. For Christian preaching places death and life in the context of the all-transforming change that has come about with the dying and rising again of Jesus Christ. Hence when that preaching speaks of death and life, it does not deal only with the basic experiences of human existence and the question of the meaning of all human destiny in general. Instead, in speaking of death and life one must speak of the very center of the Christian faith. For the Christian proclamation declares that through the death of Jesus Christ, the power of death has been laid bare and at the same time has been shattered. But what has been decided therewith, in the cross of Jesus Christ, has been manifest in the resurrection of Jesus Christ from the dead.[300] Thus in the dying and rising of Jesus Christ an event has occurred through which a totally new understanding of death and life has been disclosed.

II. The death and resurrection of Jesus Christ

a) The confession and proclamation of earliest Christianity

The content of the earliest Christian preaching is indicated by the apostle Paul at the beginning of the fifteenth chapter of his first epistle to the church at Corinth. He introduces his statements about the resurrection of the dead by reminding the Corinthians of the message that he had once brought to them and that they had received in faith. Its declarations were not formulated by the apostle himself. Instead, he had taken them over from those who were already Christians before him and had conveyed to him the message of the cross and resurrection of Jesus Christ. Since Paul explicitly states that he had handed on to the Corinthians what he on his own part had received, the tradition that he cites goes back to the very beginnings of Christianity. Its content is as follows: "that Christ died for our sins according to the Scriptures and that he was buried; that Christ was raised on the third day according to the Scriptures and that he appeared to Cephas, and then to the twelve" (1 Cor. 15:3-5).

The quotation, to which the apostle calls attention with the introduction that he has prefixed, ends at this point with verse 5. Then he begins anew and continues with the series of witnesses to whom the Resurrected One likewise has appeared, in verses 6 ff. The appropriated formulation of the one gospel by which the church lives is framed in clearly delineated phrases. Two longer statements that treat of the death and resurrection of Christ are supplemented in each case by a shorter utterance that speaks on the one hand of Jesus' tomb and on the other hand of the appearances of the resurrected one.[301]

The primitive Christian proclamation identifies the cross and resurrection of Jesus Christ as the one salvific event. For only in indissoluble interconnectedness and in the very closest reciprocal relationship are Jesus' dying and rising again rightly understood. It is because Christ was raised from the dead that his dying possesses the inherent power to achieve and to bestow salvation (1 Cor. 15:17). Without Easter, Good Friday would only signify the end of Jesus' career, and would not be able to achieve redemption and life. Nevertheless, Jesus of Nazareth is not proclaimed as the Christ in spite of the death that he had to suffer, but is confessed as the Messiah precisely because of his death. But the Crucified One did not remain in the bonds of death, but was raised on the third day. Because the resurrected and exalted Lord is identical with the historical Jesus, the Christian community does not speak solely of an event of the past. It rather announces this occurrence in the certainty that the crucified Jesus of Nazareth is the living Lord, who is proclaimed throughout all the world as the Christ of God.

That the Christ—that is, Israel's Messiah—should end his life as a wretched and suffering man on the cross, and that he died among criminals, expelled from the Holy City—this report stood in sharp conflict with the then-current messianic expectation, which had been given quite diverse formulations in the various circles of Judaism. While in the Jewish nation most people hoped for the anointed king who would appear as a

second David and would restore the glory of Israel, some
groups expected a prophet like Moses or a high priest of the
end-time who would purify Israel and prepare it for God's new
world. Quite different in appearance was the picture painted in
apocalyptic colors, which pointed to a heavenly Son of man who
would descend upon clouds and appear on the scene to judge
the ungodly and to liberate the righteous. But in spite of the
diversity among those views of the Messiah and the time of
salvation, all of them have this one thing in common: the one
anointed by God would appear as ruler and judge who would
take away the humiliation of Israel, drive out the heathen, and
establish the kingdom of splendor. Nowhere is anything said of
a suffering Messiah, who because of the sins of his people would
take upon himself humiliation and death. For where the
relationship of man to God is determined and defined solely by
the Law, where one seeks for righteousness under the Law and
knows no other way to salvation outside the divine Law, there
can be no place for a suffering Messiah who takes upon himself
the guilt of others. Hence the saying that "Christ died for our
sins" had to evoke astonishment and opposition among Jewish
hearers.

"For our sins"—this says that our sins, the alienation from
God that arose because of our sins, were the reason that the
Messiah had to suffer and die. He stepped in to fill the breach,
to do what we were not able to do. But he did this in order to
take away from us the burden, so that we might be free. That
Christ actually drank the cup of suffering to the very dregs is
underscored by the mention of the grave, "And he was buried."
Thus he died our death and was placed in a tomb, just as we all
must die and be buried.

But how could it happen that the Messiah did not appear in
splendor and glory, but gave up his life on the cross? The
Christian proclamation has always answered this question by
saying that it was God's will, that it pleased God for it to be so.
The testimony of the Scriptures is offered by way of supporting
this. "The Messiah died for our sins—according to the
Scriptures." Uppermost in thought here are certain passages in

the Old Testament that treat of the suffering and dying of a
righteous person who must endure affliction and persecution at
the hands of the ungodly. Thus Psalms 22, 31, and 69 were
repeatedly cited in connection with the account of Jesus'
passion. But it is in Isaiah 53 that we have the clearest
declarations about the suffering of the servant of God. "He bore
our griefs" (v 4); "he was wounded for our transgressions" (v 5);
"they made his grave with the ungodly" (v 9); "he will bear the
sins of many" (v 11); "he poured out his life unto death, and he
bore the sins of many" (v 12). Yet when reference is made in the
primitive Christian preaching to the Scriptures, it is not the
intention merely to lift out and emphasize individual verses or
passages of the Old Testament. Instead, significantly more is
said: the entire Scripture is understood as a witness to and for
Christ, and thus is claimed by the Christian community. For it
is only from the perspective of Christ that one rightly
understands the hitherto hidden meaning of the Scriptures.
The message of Christ is the key that provides access to their
proper interpretation.

Christ died, but on the third day God raised him from the
dead—in accordance with the Scriptures. Once again the
testimony of the Old Testament is offered in support of this
unprecedented declaration. One passage in particular could be
cited in this connection.[302] In the book of Hosea it is reported
how in their distress his contemporaries begin to seek God and
to say to each other:

> Come, let us return to the Lord;
>   for he has torn, that he may heal us;
>   he has stricken, and he will bind us up.
> After two days he will revive us;
>   on the third day he will raise us up,
>   that we may live before him.
>   (6:1-2 RSV)

Thus they cherish the expectation that after God has smitten,
then within a very short time he will lift them up again.
Actually, however, neither in the New Testament nor in the
other early Christian literature is Hosea 6:1-2 cited. Thus, in

the statement that Christ's resurrection occurred on the third day in accordance with the Scripture, there apparently was no thought of using one particular passage or another from the Old Testament as a witness for the resurrection of Jesus. Instead, just as in the case of the crucifixion, so also for the resurrection of Christ the entire Scripture was claimed as a witness.

The datum of the third day was mentioned not only in the statements of the earliest Christian preaching, but also repeatedly in the account given by the writers of the Gospels. On the one hand, it is found in the Easter narratives; early on the third day the women make their way to Jesus' tomb and discover that it is empty (Mark 16:2 and par.; John 20:1). On the other hand, this indication of time also is found in the sayings that treat of the suffering, dying, and rising again of the Son of man (Mark 8:31 and par; 9:31 and par; 10:34 and par): after three days he will rise from the dead. It is emphasized in all the primitive Christian proclamations that after a very brief time God awakened the crucified Christ from death to life.

The first witness to this message was Cephas. The earliest tradition correspondingly maintains his name (cf Luke 24:34) without relating the more specific details of the appearance of Christ which he experienced. It is not said where and how the Resurrected One appeared to him. Only the name of the witness is cited, which offers a guarantee for the truth of the declaration. Alongside him stand the Twelve who, as the most intimate group of Jesus' disciples, were together. The use of this number is meant to indicate that the entire people of God are to be gathered together as his community (cf Matt. 19:28 and par; Luke 22:30). It is not said whether they were in Galilee when the Resurrected One came to them, or whether they were still in Jerusalem. In the narratives of the Gospels, which were written later, we are told, on the one hand, that the Resurrected One appeared to his disciples in Galilee (Matt. 28:16-20), but on the other hand, it is said that he came to them while they were gathered together in Jerusalem (Luke 24:36-49; John 20:19-23). Nevertheless, the earliest Christian proclamation gives no indication of any sort as to the more specific circumstances of the event, but only cites the unprecedented occurrence as such. Christ has risen, and has appeared to Cephas and to the Twelve. Therewith they are drawn into his service as his witnesses. Their preaching stands at the beginning of the church. In many hearers it evoked an unbelieving shaking of the head, and in others even a bitter hostility. But it also found a believing agreement among those who accepted the message: that at the very place where death and the tomb appeared to have put an end to things, God has spoken the last word and has given the victory to life. It is he who gives life to the dead and calls into being that which is not (Rom. 4:17); he has demonstrated this by raising Jesus from the dead (v 24). It is only in the light of this news that the meaning of the cross of Christ can be comprehended. Hence, the primitive Christian preaching turns the direction of thought squarely around. There is no bridge that leads from death that could open the way into life. But Christ's resurrection puts death in its place. Nothing is taken away from its terrors; the cross still holds its dreadful desolateness. But death does not have the last word. The last word is spoken by God, who brings being out of nothingness and who has raised Christ from the dead. But this means that this message affects and alters the life and the death of all men. For wherever the meaning of this event is comprehended, there a new relationship to life and to death is acquired. There life is given the palm of victory and death is conquered.

b) The crucifixion of Jesus Christ

When the Christian community calls the crucified Jesus God's Messiah, it gives to this appropriated title a new meaning, which is determined by reference to the death of Jesus. The title of honor, Messiah/Christ, is always connected in the Christian proclamation with the profound humiliation through which God's Anointed One had to suffer. Hence the evangelist Mark has the confession by Peter, "You are the Christ" (Mark 8:29 and par), followed by the christological instruction, "that the Son of man must suffer many things and be rejected by the elders, chief priests, and scribes, and be killed and after three days rise again" (Mark 8:31 and par). With these words the Christian understanding of the title of Messiah is unambiguously described and interpreted by means of the story of Jesus.

This story is concisely indicated in the sayings with which the evangelists represent Jesus as solemnly predicting his sufferings, death, and resurrection. Its course is most clearly set forth in the third and last of these discourses, which the evangelist Mark places at the end of Jesus' Galilean activity. "Behold, we are going up to Jerusalem, and the Son of man will be handed over to the chief priests and the scribes, and they will condemn him to death and will hand him over to the Gentiles. And they will mock him and spit on him, and scourge him and kill him. And after three days he will rise again" (Mark 10:33-34 and par). In this sequence of events one can recognize the outline of the brief passion narrative. It begins with Jesus' arrest, then refers to the hearing before the Sanhedrin, the highest Jewish authority, then speaks of Jesus' condemnation by Pontius Pilate, and ends with his crucifixion and death. The significance of his dying, however, is understood in light of the Easter message. Christ died for our sins, and on the third day he was raised from the dead. The evangelist describes the meaning of Jesus' crucifixion with a saying of the Lord's that has been handed down to him, "The Son of man did not come to be served, but to serve and to give his life as a ransom for many" (Mark 10:45 and par). The mission and ministry of Jesus Christ are fulfilled in his having provided the ransom for all, so that they might be free.

The course of Jesus' passion would develop in such a way that the members of the Jewish high court would unite in the decision to get rid of him. The opportunity was sought and found to arrest him; a brief hearing was held, and then he was turned over to the Roman governor, that he might condemn him to death and have him executed (Mark 15:1 and par).[303] According to the unanimous accounts of the evangelists, Pilate asked Jesus whether he was the king of the Jews (Mark 15:2 and par). Behind this inquiry there is visible the accusation on account of which the Jewish authorities had handed Jesus over to the governor. Evidently Jesus was delivered into the hands of the Romans as a politically suspicious man whose preaching had aroused intolerable unrest among the populace. In this way people sought for a justification for the unreasonable demand that he be eliminated. In that process, the accusation that he had represented himself as king of the Jews could have been derived from an intentional distortion of his preaching of the dawning kingdom of God. Still the Roman ruler had to be shown, with sufficient reason, that Jesus was deserving of death. In contemporary accounts Pilate is portrayed as a cruel and ruthless governor. Hence he will not have given the matter much long thought, but will have responded promptly to the requests directed to him. Thus, after a brief trial Jesus was condemned and was nailed to the cross. In excruciating pain he died the same day.

The Christians made use of biblical language to tell of his suffering and dying. For this language alone afforded concepts and expressions with which the depth of his sufferings could be described and their meaning could be interpreted. Hence, in the passion narrative we find Old Testament quotations and allusions provided, step by step—not only in those passages where a saying from the Scripture is cited with an explicit reference, but also within the continuing narrative. In this connection, on the one hand, people have described specific episodes in the course of Jesus' passion in light of Old Testament terms—such as his being mocked, his being crucified between two malefactors, or his burial. But on the other hand, the study of the Old Testament also has led to the incorporation of individual phrases and sentences from the Psalms and the prophets into the passion narrative and these have even affected its formation. In several cases, it is no longer possible to determine with certainty whether particular statements in the passion narrative are intended to report something that happened or whether they have been taken from the reading of the Scripture and have been used to expand the narrative. Thus, it is in harmony with Psalm 69:21 that Jesus was given vinegar to drink (Mark 15:23, 26 and par). Or, again, it had already been said in Psalm 22:18 that people cast lots for the garments of a persecuted devout person (Mark 15:24 and par). It is words from the Old Testament that the dying Jesus speaks from the cross, "My God, my God, why hast thou forsaken me?" (Ps. 22:1 = Mark 15:34). This cry indeed exhibits the bitter distress that has seized the suppliant in the depth of his suffering; but precisely this desolation is given expression with a sentence from the Scripture, with which Jesus cries out to God and addresses him as "my God."

The apostle Paul says that the word of the cross is for the Jews an offense, a scandal (1 Cor. 1:23), and this means that they must stumble and fall over this word. For they demand an unequivocal sign and proof from which it can be discerned that the messianic age is actually at hand. Almost a hundred years later, the Jew Trypho confronted the Christian Justin Martyr with the fact that this so-called Christ of whom the Christians speak had been without honor and glory, so that he had even fallen victim to the worst curse that the law of God imposes; for he had been crucified (Justin, *Dialogue with Trypho the Jew* 32.1). How then could he be the Anointed One of Israel?

But to the Greeks, who seek after wisdom, after conclusive, convincing argumentation, the preaching of the cross must—as Paul comments in the same context—appear as utterly nonsensical. The gods are immortal and therefore are not subject to suffering. Whenever they appear on earth, they only put on human form like a garment which they throw off again as soon as they return to the heavenly world. It is true that the hellenistic mystery religions are acquainted with cultic myths that have been taken over from the Orient, which tell of the dying and rising of a deity. But in them there is portrayed the constantly repeated process of dying back and renewed flourishing of nature, in which suffering and death only represent the transition to new life and the appearance of salvation. The fate of the cultic deity portrays an eternal truth, not a specific historical occurrence. It is myth, not history. Therefore it remains inconceivable to the Greeks that the Son of God should have suffered and died on a cross. One must pity the Christians—so Lucian can mockingly say in the second century—for they worship as a sage a man who was executed, who in fact could be nothing but a fraud and a charlatan (*de morte Peregrini* 13). The Christians see themselves exposed to such scornful objections. The cross was everywhere regarded as a sign of shame, as the gallows on which a criminal was hanged.

No Roman citizen who was condemned to death could be executed in this shameful manner. Only slaves and revolutionaries were condemned to this dishonorable death.

We are acquainted with various signs and symbols employed by the Christians in the time of the early church. The cross, however, is not among them. A crude drawing on the wall of the Paedagogium in the Palatine in Rome must be regarded as the earliest representation of the cross of Christ.[304] There in the third century, a clumsy hand scratched on the wall a cross on which hangs a man with a donkey's head. Beneath the cross stands a man in a worshipful attitude, which is explained with the words, "Alexamenos prays to God." Undoubtedly the intention of this representation is to poke fun at a Christian. How can he pray to a deity who has revealed himself in a man who has been crucified? Scorn and ridicule are the Greeks' answer to the preaching of the cross. In the first centuries the Christians nowhere portrayed the crucifixion of Christ—this theme is absent even from the catacombs—in order not to give an advantage to a misunderstanding or a ridiculing of the gospel through a portrayal of the Crucified One. It is only from the Constantinian era onward that the sign of the cross is found as a Christian symbol, which now is intended to portray not only the suffering, but also the triumph of the lordship of Christ over the world.

In the primitive Christian proclamation people sought in various ways to explain the preaching of the crucifixion of Jesus Christ as the ground of salvation.[305] Thus the idea of sacrifice, which was universally understood in the ancient world, was utilized. God has publicly offered Christ as an expiation (Rom. 3:25). As the heavenly high priest—so the Epistle to the Hebrews teaches—Christ has offered himself as the all-sufficient sacrifice. Or again, others used the figure of a purchase or redemption, whereby a slave or a prisoner is liberated from captivity, and said, "Christ has dearly bought you, he has paid the price and has redeemed you from imprisonment" (Gal. 3:13; 4:5; 1 Cor. 6:20; 7:23). Or, again, they spoke of reconciliation, through which there is a reuniting of that which has been separated by alienation; it is said that in Christ God reconciled the world—that is, mankind, all of us—to himself (2 Cor. 5:19). Those who used these forms of expression were aware that none of them was adequate to describe in full measure the unprecedented event of the cross of Christ. None of the images employed may be stretched and forced into a dogmatic system. For if one wished to ask to whom the sacrifice of Christ was offered, there is no answer; God himself gave him up and publicly offered him as an expiatory sacrifice. What sense is there in saying that Christ functions as the high priest and at the same time in this ministry presents himself as the sacrifice? And to whom is the price that Christ provided in the redemption supposed to have been paid? One cannot think of Satan in this connection, since the satanic power is set in opposition to the sufferings of Christ and seeks to prevent them (Mark 8:33 and par). But further, God cannot be represented as the one who receives the price. For it is not men that provide the price that is paid, but God himself acts in giving up Christ in our stead. He alone achieves the reconciliation. Nowhere in the New Testament is it said that God has been reconciled, but it is constantly emphasized that God, and no one else, performs the work of reconciliation by coming to us in Christ. Therefore the customary expressions about sacrifice, redemption, and reconciliation do not serve to establish or to develop a doctrinal system. Instead, what they intend is nothing other than to emphasize ever anew the unprecedented news that God in his incomprehensible love has turned toward us, in giving up Christ to the cross. Death puts an end to the life of every man, closes his mouth, and silences him. But Jesus' dying speaks, because he rose from the dead, and the cross-event is proclaimed as the proof of the unfathomable mercy of God. Therewith death is deprived of its power to separate one from God and to destroy life. Jesus remained in the very closest devotion to God to the very last. But that is not all; by raising him from the dead, God has uttered his yes to him and confirmed the cross as the proof of his love. But thereby fellowship with God in the midst of suffering and death is made available to all men. Therefore anyone who trusts in the cross of Christ likewise is not abandoned by God in death.[306] The apostle Paul says that on the cross the unheard-of exchange took place. For our sake God "made him to be sin who knew no sin, so that in him we might become the righteousness of God" (2 Cor. 5:21 RSV). This means that Christ was so utterly covered by the burden that he had taken upon himself that there was no longer anything to be seen of him but the sin with which he was burdened. But thereby he has taken it away and has brought us into a right relationship with God. Paul formulates it even more sharply in the Epistle to the Galatians. The word of Scripture that "cursed is everyone who hangs on a tree" (Deut. 21:23) applies to Christ; for he became accursed for us (Gal. 3:13). He was affected in its full force by the curse of estrangement from God—in our place, on our behalf. Therefore at the cross, the power of the divine blessing was released, applying to Jews and Gentiles alike—to all who believe.

In the crucifixion of Jesus Christ—the author of the Fourth Gospel tells us—the aim of the Father's sending the Son was fulfilled. The eternal Word became man, in order that, suffering and dying, he might perfect his work. According to the Gospel of John, Jesus' last utterance was "It is finished." Then he bowed his head and died (John 19:30). The Crucified One had fulfilled his commission and thus with great sublimity surrendered his life. Just as Moses once had lifted up the serpent so that all who looked to it might be delivered, so was it necessary for the Son of man to be lifted up (John 3:14). But being lifted up means two things at the same time: to be nailed to the cross that is erected on the hill Golgotha, and thereby to be glorified.[307] Hence Good Friday and Easter come together in the cross-event. "God so loved the world that he gave his only Son, that whoever believes in him should not be lost, but should have eternal life" (John 3:16). But this proclamation can be comprehended only by a person who lets himself be addressed as a sinner, one who in light of the cross of Christ acknowledges that he is lost and in view of the Crucified One recognizes him as the Lord who receives and accepts those who are lost.

c) The resurrection of Jesus Christ

Christ's resurrection[308] cannot be compared with awakening of a deceased person through which that person is brought back to life and once again is subjected to the circumstances and conditions of life until he dies again. For Christ did not come back into this life, but pressed his way through death to life. Hence, the Easter-event is proclaimed as a victory over death and a breakthrough into life. A compelling proof of the truth of this message cannot be produced, but the Easter testimony of the first disciples demonstrates its truth by its own power, and it continues to live in the church's preaching.[309] Faith alone is able to comprehend that Christ is the living Lord. Hence, there is no one who could have reported an appearance of the Resurrected One from a stance of critical detachment. The people to whom the Resurrected One was attested as the Lord were without exception taken into his service, not only Cephas and the Twelve, but also the others whom Paul cites as witnesses of the Resurrected One.

After the appearances to Cephas and the Twelve—so the testimony reads—the Resurrected One appeared to more than five hundred brethren (1 Cor. 15:6). Nothing is said about where and how this appearance took place. Paul only adds that most of them were still living, though some of them had already died. What is this comment supposed to signify? No Christian—not even in the Corinthian community that was torn by tensions and disputes—would have doubted that Christ had risen from the dead. Therefore, there was no need of explicit information; one could get more specific details from those witnesses of the Resurrected One who were still alive. What was surprising to the early Christians, who were anticipating the imminent return of Christ at the last day, was rather that there were deaths occurring, that members of the infant community were dying before the dawning of God's new world. Paul mentions that some of those who have seen the risen Christ have in the meantime fallen asleep, and in making this comment he notes that those who are deceased are removed from the circle of the witnesses of the Resurrected One.[310] This makes it evident that the resurrection of Christ is not discernible as a present event, but rather lies in a historical past, which of course now exerts a definitive influence upon the total life of the Christians.[311] It is the apostle's intent to call the Corinthians' attention to this fact.

The enumeration then is continued in chronological order.

Then the Resurrected One appeared to James and to all the apostles (1 Cor. 15:7). James, the brother of the Lord, had remained aloof during Jesus' lifetime, but then had very early joined the Jerusalem community and had later taken over its leadership. There is no more reported about the circumstances of this appearance than in the reference to the apostles. The latter apparently may not be equated with the Twelve, who had already been mentioned; instead, the term "apostles" refers to a particular group of primitive Christian missionaries who had been commissioned for service by the risen Christ. At the end, Paul lists himself as the last one to whom the Resurrected One had revealed himself (v 8). This concludes the series. Since Paul earlier had persecuted the community and then had changed from being an opponent of the Christians into a preacher of the gospel, the example of his being called makes it manifest that God's grace has been proven effective in him, and consequently there is such a thing as Christian existence solely on the basis of the divine mercy (v 9-10).[312] Nevertheless, Paul nowhere describes the appearance of the Resurrected One that he had experienced—in contradistinction to the legendary formulation of the story of his call in Acts 9, 22, and 26—but only refers to the event as such: God had revealed his Son to him (Gal. 1:16); he had seen the Lord (1 Cor. 9:1).

The Easter message, which is summarized in the brief statement that God has raised Christ from the dead, stands at the beginning of all Christian proclamation. It is more ancient than the Easter narratives recorded in the Gospels. While the earliest proclamation exclusively cites the "that" of Christ's resurrection, the Easter narratives offer a later deposit of the Easter preaching by which it was supposed to be made vivid. In matters of detail these stories rather significantly diverge from each other, and they are not historical accounts, but are descriptive presentations of the proclamation of the Resurrected One. The evangelists Mark and Matthew presuppose the Galilean Easter tradition (Mark 14:28 and par; 16:7 and par), according to which the Resurrected One appeared to his disciples in Galilee and gave them the commission to preach among all the nations (Matt. 28:16-20). In and Gospel of Luke, on the other hand, the Easter stories are localized in and near

Jerusalem (Luke 24:15-53). Here the Holy City is emphasized as the connecting link which is determined by the history of Israel, and through which the continuity is established between the Old Testament people of God, the history of Jesus, and the career of the church, which had its beginning in Jerusalem. In the Gospel of John, the two strands of tradition are bound together. In chapter 20, with which the book originally ended, the Jerusalem Easter tradition is accepted (v 30-31). And in the added chapter 21, Galilean appearances are related. The diverse traditions are finally bound together in the secondary conclusion to Mark's Gospel, into a kind of harmony of the Gospels which briefly summarizes the various Easter stories.[313]

A special position among the Easter stories is held by the account of the discovery of the empty tomb (Mark 16:1-8 and par).[314] Early on Easter morning some women came to Jesus' tomb to anoint his body. They found the tomb empty, and heard from the mouth of an angel the message: "You seek Jesus of Nazareth, who was crucified. He has risen, he is not here" (Mark 16:6 RSV). In the earliest Christian proclamation, the reference to Jesus' having been buried belonged to the declaration that treated of Christ's death, not of his resurrection (1 Cor. 15:4). It was meant to underscore the fact that he had taken suffering and death upon himself, to the very end. In the accounts in the Gospels, on the other hand, the tomb is brought into connection with the Easter message. The discovery of the empty tomb is supposed to be understood as an indication of the resurrection of Christ. Nevertheless, the evangelists refrain from picturing the resurrection of Jesus itself. It is not until the apocryphal Gospel of Peter that the attempt is first made to describe it. There it is said:

> But in the night in which the Lord's day was dawning, when the soldiers were standing watch two by two, there sounded a loud voice in heaven. And they saw the heavens opened and two men in great brilliance come down from there and approach the tomb. But that stone that had been placed against the mouth of the sepulchre started to roll of its own accord and moved to one side. And the sepulchre was opened, and the two young men entered in. Now when those

soldiers saw this, they awakened the centurion and the elders—for they too were there keeping watch. And while they were telling what they had seen, they saw again three men coming out of the tomb, two of them supporting the third, and a cross following them; and the heads of the two reached up to the heavens, but the head of him whom they led by the hand towered above the heavens. And they heard a voice from heaven calling, "Have you preached to those who have fallen asleep?" And an answer was heard from the cross, "Yes." Then they consulted with each other about going and reporting this to Pilate. And while they were still debating, the heavens were seen to open again, and a man descended and entered into the sepulchre.

While this presentation seeks to satisfy curiosity by penetrating the mystery and aims at the beholding of the resurrection, the evangelists convey only the word of the proclamation. For they know that the resurrection of Jesus Christ from the dead remains hidden from our eyes. What really matters is rather the word of the good news. Only in the Gospel of Matthew there is a brief allusion to the fact that a great earthquake occurred, and an angel had come down from heaven and rolled away the stone (Matt. 28:2-3). Yet even in Matthew the emphasis rests on the saying that the angel addresses to the women: "I know that you are seeking Jesus, who was crucified. He is not here, for he has risen, as he said" (28:5-6). The evangelists are well aware that the empty tomb cannot offer any conclusive proof; for people could also assert that Jesus' disciples had stolen his body (Matt. 28:11-15). The content of the Easter message is unequivocally defined only through the word that proclaims the Resurrected One.

The story of the two disciples who encountered the Resurrected One on the road to Emmaus is especially vividly formulated (Luke 24:13-35). Faith is established through the encounter with Jesus the Christ. He is the center of the entire Scripture, which from the first word to the last bears witness to him (24:26-27, 32). When the Scripture is rightly read and interpreted, then from it the word of the Resurrected One is perceived, so that his community comprehends: it is in keeping with God's will that Christ had to suffer, and out of his suffering to enter into glory.

The Christian faith confesses the one declaration: "God has raised him from the dead" (Rom. 10:9) Therewith in a few words there is declared the deed of God through which he awakened life out of death, and called it into being out of nothingness. This belief in the Resurrected One is expressed in the multiplicity of the Easter stories. In their many-voiced choir, however, only the one testimony is intended to be made clear: God has raised him from the dead. That miracle wrought by God cannot be grasped by our minds; it is announced exclusively in the testimony of the witnesses. But its effects are clearly to be seen, and they are not hidden, even to the opponents of the Christian faith. The people to whom the Easter message comes are divided into believers and nonbelievers. While those of one group think that they are to trust only whatever in this world they can seize and have at their disposal, the others set their hope solely on the promise of God, which he has validated in the resurrection of Jesus Christ from the dead. But from the confession that the Christian faith utters there follows the confident hope of the Christians: "God has raised the Lord, and he will also raise us up by his power" (1 Cor. 6:14).

III. The victory over death

a) The God of the living

The question of what lies beyond death has always concerned men. Where may this journey lead? And to what goal is the way of man directed? In Platonic philosophy the answer is given that death indeed affects the body and delivers it over to decay, but thereby the soul is liberated from the prison in which it was confined. This teaching also found its way into circles of hellenistic Judaism, which sought to harmonize the biblical tradition with ideas of Greek philosophy. The devout person knew that he was destined for heavenly fulfillment, and therefore he lived in accordance with God's commandment, so that in due time his soul would be taken into the heavenly world. Yet neither the writings of the Old Testament nor Palestinian Judaism had the idea of an immortal soul of man which at the end of the earthly life would be set free from the body that enveloped it.[315] Man is rather regarded as a unitary being which, with his body and soul, his members and mind, was created by God to live in accordance with the will of his creator. His time is set for him, and at the end of his way he must die. The man who trusts in God and who in his conduct adheres to God's word stands, in his entire life, in a relationship of closeness to his God.

Precisely in suffering and affliction the devout person places his hope solely in God. Hence, it was necessary to ask the question whether this relationship ends at the hour of death, or whether it reaches beyond death. Will the God who guides his own people through the dark valley also stand at the far end of this way? This question, which sounds again and again in the prayers and the psalms of the Old Testament, yearns for an affirmative answer, which then found its expression in the hope of the resurrection of the dead. In the harsh struggles which the Jews had to endure in the second century B.C., struggles against Syrian and hellenistic foreign domination, they were beset by the question whether the righteous ones who had fallen in battle would also share in the future salvation. A solution was first sought in the expectation that individual pious persons from Israel's history and the martyrs would be raised from the dead in order to share in full blessedness (2 Macc. 7). Those who fear God will arise to eternal life, while the sinners will fall victim to corruption and will never more be raised (Ps. Sol. 3:10-12).

Soon, however, the idea of the resurrection, in connection with the world judgment that was portrayed in apocalyptic, was expanded to say that not only would the righteous rise to a life of blessedness, but all men would be raised from death to stand before the judgment bar of God. Now it is said that all the dead, the ungodly as well as the righteous, will be raised at the last judgment (see above, pp 83ff). The only exceptions are the sinners who have been murdered, who through their death have already sufficiently atoned for their guilt and therefore no longer have any need to appear before the judgment bar. The so-called Similitudes, in Ethiopic Enoch 37–71, the visions of the apocalypse of Ezra, and the Syriac apocalypse of Baruch (30:1-5; 50:2–51:3) then presuppose the general resurrection of all the dead. At the end of time the earth must give up the dead that rest in her, so that they may rise from the graves and appear before the throne of the Most High. In this perspective the process of the resurrection is uniformly conceived of as a bodily reawakening of the dead, who are raised up again in the same earthly form in which they once lived, and now must answer for their deeds that they earlier committed. Thereby the identity of the resurrected person with the one who had died is assured, so that this person has to give an accounting for all that he once did. After the sentence of judgment, which God as the eternal judge pronounces, the righteous enter into bliss, and the condemned are sent away into the underworld.[316]

While the expectation of the resurrection of the dead is derived from the question whether the fellowship of the devout with their God will continue beyond death, still the development of this conception cannot be explained solely from the further unfolding of beginnings within the Old Testament and Jewish piety. Instead, Iranian influences, with which the Jewish community came into contact particularly during the Babylonian exile and the period that followed this (see pp 86ff, above), contributed to it. By means of the hope that God would call forth the dead from their tombs and would gather his people about him, vivid expression could be given to the assurance that his faithfulness would abide forever. The idea here is not that there resides in man a divine "I" that must be liberated by death in order to return to God. Instead, it was the idea of God that was solely determinative. Man must die, and he remains subject to death. But God's faithfulness remains and does not abandon those who are his. He will raise them out of death and will lead them to eternal life.

In the time of Jesus and of earliest Christianity this conviction was shared by many Jews in Palestine. It was held particularly by the Pharisees, who enjoyed high esteem among the people and were widely regarded as examples of pious and righteous living. Their view was contradicted by the Sadducees, whose numbers included preeminently the priestly nobility of Jerusalem and circles of the leading families in the capital city. These appealed to the ancient teaching that man must die and must find in death his irrevocable end, and they ridiculed the idea that the dead would rise again. For would what had once happened here perhaps reoccur in the world beyond?

This ironic objection was advanced by some Sadducees who challenged Jesus to debate (Mark 12:18-27 and par). They based their argument upon Scripture. The Old Testament prescribes that when a man dies without offspring, his brother should take the widow to himself and marry her, in order to provide descendants for his deceased brother (Deut. 25:5-6). Now a case is constructed which, to be sure, strikes one as improbable, but is formulated in such a way that it is supposed to refute the expectation of a resurrection. There were seven brothers. The first of them took a wife, and soon thereafter died without leaving children. Then the second brother took the widow as his wife. But he too soon died without having a child. The same thing happened with the third, and so on through all the rest, to the seventh. Now this example is followed by the question; How will it be in the resurrection of the dead? Then the dead are to be awakened and to appear before God's judgment seat as the same persons they had been during their lifetime. But whose then is the wife who had been married to seven men in succession? She had conducted herself as the scriptural commandment had directed her, and complied with the prescriptions of the so-called levirate marriage. On the basis of this example, must not the conception of a resurrection of the dead appear mistaken? And what is the life of those who are raised from the dead going to be like after all?

The point of beginning and the line of argument in this debate are skillfully chosen. Must not the idea that the dead are to be wakened to life in fact be regarded as foolish? But you are wrong, Jesus answers the Sadducees. You are making your judgment on the basis of utterly mistaken assumptions, and therefore you neither grasp the meaning of what is in the Scripture nor are even able to imagine what God's power can do. For the resurrection of the dead does not bring with it an extension in the hereafter of relationships of the present world. In the resurrection of the dead there will be neither marriage nor giving in marriage, but those who are raised will be like the angels in heaven. What does this mean? In God's world things will not be as they are on earth. Therefore it may not be inferred from earthly relationships that conditions hereafter could or must be such-and-such. Any attempt to think of the resurrection of the dead in this way in fact is shown to be inappropriate. Then, everything will be entirely different. Hence anyone who tries to assert, by means of cleverly chosen arguments, that there cannot be a resurrection of the dead may indeed be able to exhibit evidence of his own keenness of mind. But precisely thereby he shows that he does not at all know who God is. For resurrection of the dead can neither be conceived of on the basis of the nature of man nor grounded in the possibilities of the structures of human life. Instead, what the resurrection of the dead is can only be comprehended at all when one speaks of God's deity, his power, and his glory.

After the Sadducees' objection is refuted in this fashion, there is added the positive argument whereby the hope of the resurrection of the dead is justified. Like the objection, it is taken from the Old Testament and, like it, from the books of Moses. In the Scripture we read: "I am the God of Abraham, the God of Isaac, and the God of Jacob" (Exod. 3:6). With this statement the God of Israel reveals himself to be the one whom the fathers had followed and to whom now Moses and the nation were in like manner to belong. From the Old Testament saying now the inference is drawn: God is not a God of the dead, but of the living (see p 54-55). Therewith a principle was adopted which had been formulated by Jewish scribes and had been frequently employed. Where God is, death cannot be. With him is life, not death; being, not decay. For when God names the names of the patriarchs Abraham, Isaac, and Jacob, he indicates thereby that he not only *was* their God, but also *is* their God. But then it must be true that "to him, all are alive" (Luke 20:38). God does not abandon his own; he stands by his word and calls them out of death into life. Because God is the God of the living, there is therefore a resurrection of the dead.

Just how things may happen then need not be discussed. There is no necessity of a graphic description. No indication is given whether we shall once again see those who were near to us here. It is only God's deity that is spoken of here. Whoever is with him is in life. To know this is sufficient. But anyone who does not comprehend what is said here, who wants to debate the matter, to calculate or to dispute the possibilities, is ensnared in profoundest error. For the crux of the matter still is the only positive rationale for the belief in the resurrection of the dead: "God is not a God of the dead, but of the living."

The question of the fate of the dead aroused some disturbance in the earliest Christian communities. They were filled with the expectation that this world would not long stand but would soon pass away and give place to God's new world. Then Christ would appear on the clouds of heaven, hold judgment over the living and the dead, and bring in the splendor of the kingdom of God. But this longed-for day was delayed. Instead of its appearance, death intervened in the life of the communities. Thus was posed the urgent question whether the deceased Christians would have a share in the coming salvation, or whether they were excluded from it. Devout Jews also had similarly asked whether the servants of God who had departed before the beginning of the end-time could share in the experience of what will happen in the time of redemption. "Woe to those who do not remain"—thus cried one of the seers (4 Ezra 13:16). For they could not behold what would happen to Israel then. How then is it with the dead who have departed before the day of Christ's return has dawned? What will their fate be, and what hope is there for them?

In the first epistle to the church at Thessalonica the apostle Paul gives an answer to this question. This church had arisen through Paul's missionary activity and had developed well. But then the apostle had been obliged to leave the city and was unable to continue with the building-up of the community. Soon after the separation, some deaths had occurred, and had confronted the Christian hope with a severe test. For would not one have to fear that the deceased would not share in the experience of Christ's royal advent? In order to do away with this anxiety, Paul enters into these questions that have arisen in the Thessalonian community and writes that he does not want to leave the community in ignorance about the fate of those who have fallen asleep (1 Thess. 4:13-18).[317] Using the manner of speaking that was current in the hellenistic environment, he speaks of the deceased as those who are asleep. This expression, however, was not meant to deny or to limit the reality of death. Instead, it was common then as it is now to speak of dying with the less harsh term of falling asleep. Nevertheless, men stand helpless—so Paul says—in the face of the reality of death. For they can only continue in grief, because they ultimately have no hope. But in contrast to this, the Christians know, by the power of their faith, that death does not signify the end, because Christ has triumphed over death. Hence there follows from the content of their faith the certainty that God will bring with him those who have fallen asleep with Jesus—that is, as Christians (v 14). Thus all those who have died in faith in Christ cannot be torn from their position of belonging to their Lord, but they will be raised and will be included in the triumphal procession in which he will visibly appear at the end. To provide justification for this idea, Paul appeals to a saying of the Lord, which he cites and ornaments with explanatory comments.

In this connection the apostle relies on a train of thought that was handed down to him and to the communities orally. For at the time of the composition of the epistle—about A.D. 50 there were no written gospels. The Gospel of Mark was only written shortly before A.D. 70, and the other Gospels in the following decades. What was known about Jesus in the time of the apostle Paul was handed on in the communities by word of mouth. This tradition also contained sayings that deal with the last times and the coming of the Lord in judgment and for the redemption of his people. In this process people also appropriated individual utterances that had developed in the eschatological expectations of Judaism. The saying of the Lord that Paul mentions to the Thessalonians belongs to this context of the hope that is oriented to the coming change. The liveliness of this hope is demonstrated by the fact that Paul counts himself among those who will still be alive at that day. Thus the coming of Christ would occur within so short a time. Then—so the apostle emphasizes—those who are still alive will not have an advantage over those who have died. Instead, it will be like this: "For the Lord himself will descend from heaven with a cry of command, with the archangel's call, and with the sound of the trumpet of God. And the dead in Christ will rise first; then we who are alive, who are left, shall be caught up together with them in the clouds to meet the Lord in the air; and so we shall always be with the Lord" (1 Thess. 4:16-17 RSV). The formulation of this quotation has been stamped by the confession and the believing expectation of the Christian community. Hence, it speaks of the Lord in whom the community believes, of his ceremonial advent, and of the dead in Christ. But the language of Jewish apocalyptic also provides the references to the cry of command, the voice of the archangel, the trumpets that will announce the judgment, and the coming of the judge of the world, who will appear from heaven. But in contrast to the apocalyptic descriptions of the eschatological events, the features that are cited here offer no more precise description of the course of events in the end. They serve only as brief references to the coming of the Lord, and are meant to emphasize the crucially important utterance: Christ will appear as Lord, will call forth the deceased Christians from their graves, and will combine them, with the community of the living, into his people. Then together they will go to meet the Lord. This picture is borrowed from the customary practice in antiquity, that when the Roman emperor made a visit to a city, the citizens would go outside the gate to escort the exalted guest inside the walls in a ceremonial procession. Thus, also all who belong to Christ will greet him as the coming ruler and then will be privileged to abide with him forever. With this statement the apostle's answer to the community's question is given its crowning conclusion.

In spite of the fact that the language of apocalyptic is unmistakable in these sentences, yet remarkably little use is made of it.[318] Apocalyptic conceptions are only barely mentioned, in order to characterize the eschatological hope with simple, spare words. At the center, however, stands the christological declaration. Hence, the author can refrain from any sort of amplification and depiction of the future glory. It is sufficient to know that those who belong to the Lord will always be with him; all other considerations pale into insignificance in comparison with this. There are no speculations offered, either concerning the secret background of the history that has already occurred or concerning the course of future happenings, but the gaze is only turned forward—toward the future and the coming of the Lord, in whom God, who has raised Christ from the dead, will be attested as the God of the living.

b) The resurrection of the dead

In the church of Corinth the hope of the resurrection of the dead, which was shared by Jews and Christians, was called into question. "There is no resurrection of the dead"; this thesis summed up the refutation that some were advancing (1 Cor. 15:12). What reflections in particular are concealed behind this denial is not wholly clear.

The background of that sharp dispute must be deduced—insofar as this is possible at all—from the line of argument with which the apostle engages the Corinthians in debate. How can Christians say that there is no resurrection of the dead? For there is no doubt that the Corinthians intended to be Christians and had no intention of abandoning their faith. But then they will also have agreed with the statement that Christ has been raised from the dead, and is the living Lord. Only with this assumption does it become comprehensible that Paul sets out from this conviction common to all Christians, and places at the beginning of his declarations the primitive Christian gospel of Christ's cross and resurrection (1 Cor. 15:3-5). He intends therewith to describe the foundation upon which all Christians stand and which even the Corinthians did not intend to abandon. But what follows from this statement of the confession? What does it mean for the outlook which a Christian acquires for his life?

Apparently some in Corinth had adopted the view that with the resurrection of Christ the powers of the new world had already become effective. Anyone who believed in Christ and had been baptized into him was grasped and renewed by these powers, so that he was permeated by the power of the Spirit and was transported into blessedness. It is not only in the future, but already in the present, as it is experienced in the Christian community, that salvation is here and now actualized. This is the reason Paul addresses the community with his ironic question; apparently they have already been definitively satisfied, have become truly rich, and have already been transported into the kingdom of God, while the apostle does not share in such blessedness but must endure persecution and suffering (Cor. 4:8-13). But there is something out of rhyme here. The fanatical enthusiasm that has seized the Corinthians carries them beyond the sober reality in which a Christian must live and causes them to adopt the erroneous opinion that consummation and perfection had already arrived.

Toward the end of the first century A.D. there were people in some communities who announced the opinion that the resurrection had already occurred (2 Tim. 2:18). Where a person is inclined toward such an opinion, of course one can then declare that there cannot be a resurrection of the dead that will occur in the future. It cannot be determined with certainty whether this doctrine in this form had already been set forth in Corinth as well. However, it is altogether conceivable that similar views were in fact already present among the Corinthians.[319] Such a teaching, however, had to lead to a low estimate of the responsibilities of everyday living and to the view that it does not matter how one conducts oneself. For if one holds the view that the state of blessedness has already arrived, then one can claim that anything is permissible (1 Cor. 6:12; 10:23), and it does not matter whether a Christian enters into relations with a prostitute (1 Cor. 6:12-20), or whether one decides to remain unmarried (1 Cor. 7:1-40). Then one can observe the Lord's Supper as a feast of the blessed, and not pay any attention to whether poor members of the community, who are unable to bring any food or who can arrive only after the observance has begun, receive anything (1 Cor. 11:18-32). But do Christians who think in this way actually understand what the resurrection of Christ means for their lives?

The apostle must pose this weighty question to the Corinthians. Certainly the power of the Spirit, which God has imparted to those who are his, has made a fundamental change in their lives. But the Spirit is not yet the consummation, but is, as it were, the down payment, which as the deposit paid in advance validly guarantees the glory that is to come (2 Cor. 1:22; 5:5). That glory has not yet arrived, but it is confidently anticipated by the believers. With Christ's resurrection the end of time has dawned, but it is not yet fulfilled. Therefore the Christians who remain faithful to their Lord are on their way, and they find themselves on the pilgrimage between the times. They come from the resurrection of Christ, which places its mark and stamp upon their lives and their conduct. And they are going toward the future resurrection of the dead through which their hope is to be actualized. A Christian therefore cannot and may not act with indifference toward the demands of the day or toward the fate of his brothers. Because he knows that God, who has raised the Lord, will also raise us by his power (1 Cor. 6:14), he does not have free rein even over his own body, to use it and to act however it pleases him. Instead, his body—all that he is or has, does or refrains from doing—belongs to the Lord (1 Cor. 6:13).

The apostle carries through his discussion with the views of the Corinthians in the following manner: in the first part of the train of thought, he treats the affirmation *that* the dead rise, because indeed otherwise the preaching of the resurrection of Christ could not be true (1 Cor. 15:12-34). Then in a second phase he sets forth *how* the dead are raised and how the entrance into the kingdom of God will occur (v 35-38). In this process he takes up in each phase one of the arguments of the Corinthians and seeks to deprive it of its force by recalling again and again that the Christian faith confesses the Crucified and Risen One as the Lord (Rom. 10:9). For from this confession it must necessarily be inferred that the statement that there is no resurrection of the dead can in no wise be harmonized with the belief in the resurrected Christ. But whoever believes that Christ died and rose again also knows that the dead who have fallen asleep in Christ will be raised and will be with their Lord.

How can the resurrection of the dead be established and justified as the content of the Christian faith and Christian hope? In answering this question the apostle adduces neither general considerations nor reflections such as were set forth in the eschatological expectations of Judaism. Instead, he presupposes that he is addressing Christians who are ready to reflect upon the content and the consequences of Christian preaching. Hence it is unnecessary to undertake the hardly promising attempt to find arguments that could appear irrefutable to anyone and everyone. Instead, Paul refers decisively to the principle that Christ is preached as the one who has been raised from the dead. Thus to speak of the resurrection of the dead means to apply the preaching of Christ to the Christians' own living and dying. For it is not wishes or vague hopes of men, but only belief in Christ, who has risen from the dead, that justifies and supports the confidence that God will raise the dead.[320] But from this consideration it then follows: "But if it is preached of Christ that he rose from the dead, how then do some among you say that there is no resurrection of the dead" (1 Cor. 15:12). If they agree that Christ is the risen Lord, then they cannot deny that the dead are raised. Otherwise that would mean that even Christ cannot have been raised.

If there is no resurrection of the dead, then Christ too cannot have been raised. Paul twice (v 13 and 16) emphasizes this negative conclusion, and each time he connects with it a special observation. The first refers to the preaching of the apostle (vv 14-15), and the second to the faith of the community (vv 17-18). Thus if the content of the Christian confession is doubted, the preaching is hollow and empty (v 14). But then its preachers would be people who do not deserve to be believed. For then they would have shown themselves to be—knowingly or perhaps even unknowingly—false witnesses, who have not spoken trustworthily. Then they would have asserted that God has raised Christ from the dead when in fact he had not done so (v 15). But who is there who wants to make this monstrous accusation against the apostles?

Yet it is not only the preachers, but also the hearers of the Christian proclamation who would be very gravely affected if it were actually true that there is no resurrection of the dead, and consequently even Christ cannot have been raised. Then the faith of the Christians, who have accepted the message of Christ, would have to be idle and without any content (v 17). For therewith, not only would the Easter message actually be robbed of its content, but there would no longer be any saving significance in the cross of Christ. Christ's death then perhaps would be the end of a noble man who, through courageous behavior or silent submission in his unavoidable fate, earned the respect of those who observed his death. But no redemptive power could issue from this end. For only because the Crucified One was raised from the dead is his cross a valid guarantee that he has taken our place, has assumed and carried our burden, so that the dominion of sin is broken. Hence Paul expresses the conclusion that would unavoidably have to be drawn in these words: "But if Christ is not risen . . . you are yet in your sins" (v 17). Since in this passage the apostle does not speak of sin in the singular but of a number of sinful deeds, he does not follow here his own customary usage but adopts the primitive Christian manner of expression that antedated his time. Thereby Paul indicates that in the reflections which he sets forth as conceivable possibilities he is expounding the confessional utterance that had been handed down to him and to the community. Do the Corinthians actually wish to stand by their thesis that there is no resurrection of the dead? The probing question lays bare the seriousness of the problem, which earlier had hardly been made clear to them. Anyone who says that there can be no resurrection of the dead not only thereby does away with the resurrection of Christ but also takes away from the cross its meaning. But then also those who have fallen asleep trusting in Christ would be lost. For their faith, too, would be demonstrated to be idle and null. This holds true for them as for all Christians (v 18). If the content of the Christian hope were to relate to nothing other than this life, then indeed we would be the most wretched among all men (v 19). For then the faith and hope of the Christians would not be capable of leading them beyond misery, distress, and death. Instead, they would relapse into abandonment and hopelessness and could not be brought out again from that plight.

The only appropriate manner of discourse in which one can speak of the resurrection of Jesus Christ is the proclamation which announces the Risen One as the living Lord. Therefore in his premise Paul can say one time, "But if Christ is preached as having been raised from the dead" (v 12), and another time,

"If Christ has (or has not) been raised" (vv 14, 17), without introducing any difference into the meaning of the expression. Thus, in either case Paul draws the conclusions that would have to follow from the Corinthian thesis for Christian preaching and the Christian faith. In so doing he remains faithful to his point of beginning, which he adopted in preaching Christ, and does not speak of all humanity, but only of the Christians and of those who have fallen asleep in Christ and who belong to the risen Lord. General considerations as to what could become of the whole of humanity are not introduced. Any and all speculation is left aside, for his concern is to speak of death and life as it is necessary now to speak of them under the sign of the cross and resurrection of Jesus Christ.

What follows now from this point of departure that the apostle has chosen for his discussion? In the following passage Paul discusses the indissoluble connection between Christ's resurrection and the resurrection of the dead (v 20-28). He dismisses with a wave of the hand that theoretically posed possibility that there could be no resurrection of the dead and hence no resurrection of Christ. It does not come into serious consideration at all. For Christ has in fact risen from the dead, as the firstfruits of those who have fallen asleep (v 20). With this expression Paul refers to the custom, prescribed in the Old Testament, of bringing the firstfruits and sheaves from the harvest to the priest, as a sign that the produce of the land belongs to the God of Israel (Lev. 23:10). The gift of the firstfruits was meant to indicate that everything belongs to God. When Christ now is called the firstfruits, this is meant to say that as the Resurrected One he stands for the whole of humanity. With Christ's resurrection, the resurrection of the dead has already begun. For the first one has risen from the dead, but the others will be raised. Hence Christ's resurrection signifies nothing less than the beginning of the resurrection of the dead. In order to make evident the universal breadth and scope of this event, the apostle explains that statement by contrasting Adam and Christ, to whom he also refers in the context of the exposition of the message of Christ in Romans 5:12-21. In that exposition, the reader's gaze is turned from the Christ-event back to the past, and there is a full acknowledgment of the unavoidability of the fate of death that hangs over all men and can be broken only by Christ. Through one man—Adam—came death, so that all men must die. But through one man also comes the resurrection of the dead. For this now is the sequence: As in Adam all men must die, and even Christians are not spared from physical death, so in Christ shall all be made alive—that is, all who in faith confess him, who have fallen asleep in Christ, and who cling to the assured hope that Christ will not abandon those who are his (vv 21-22). Although in this passage it is said in only a few words by way of allusion, the crucial difference is not overlooked. While from Adam's deed there issued an unavoidable necessity from which no man could escape, resurrection and life, which Christ brings, are imparted to those who believe in him (cf Rom. 5:12-21).

Christ's resurrection has already occurred, but the resurrection of the dead lies before us as a future event. Paul speaks specifically of a sequence of the eschatological event: each one in his own order, first of all Christ, the firstfruits, then those who belong to Christ, who are to be raised at Christ's coming (v 23), and then comes the end (v 24). And this end means that Christ will hand over the rule to God the Father. Then everything will be placed in God's hands, and all the powers and forces of darkness will be defeated and set aside. Christ's rule will last—so it is read from Psalm 110:1—until the day when all enemies have been put under his feet. The last enemy, who still holds sway but at the end will be conquered and destroyed, is death (v 26). Thus death is still present, and eternal blessedness has not yet arrived. Therewith Paul refutes the opinion of the Corinthians that they could already give themselves over to the rapture of the blessed. In holding that opinion they are overlooking the reality of death, which as a hostile power still threatens the lives of men and awaits even the Christians. But there is victory over death only where Christ is. Therefore anyone who clings to Christ and whom Christ holds is allied with the one who will in all events be victorious in the struggle with death. But when the last enemy has been disarmed, God alone will remain on the scene, and he will be all in all (v 28). Then there will be no more death, but only life. This event, which leads to the ultimate annihilation of death, thus has already been initiated. The future has already begun with the resurrection of Jesus Christ from the dead.

Paul had said in verse 19 that Christian life in which there is only a hope that is limited to this world would be wretched and pitiable. Now he comes back to this idea once again and points out to his adversaries that Christian faith without hope in the resurrection of the dead would be robbed of its content and its meaning. Actually, even the Corinthians by no means conducted themselves as consistently as their words perhaps would have required. For in actuality they demonstrated that even among them there was a hope that extended beyond death, by their curious practice of a baptism for the dead. Paul mentions this practice only in passing, in order to call the Corinthians' attention to the contradictory nature of their behavior. Other than this, he does not devote a single word to describing the practice, nor does he adopt a critical stance with reference to it. Apparently what was involved was a custom like the one that also existed in later centuries in some groups that had separated themselves from the Great Church.[321] If someone who desired baptism died without receiving it, another person would be concealed beneath the bier of the deceased. This person then would answer in the affirmative to the question whether he wished to be baptized, and would then be baptized on behalf of the deceased, who then was supposed to receive the benefits of baptism. Where such a baptism for the dead is performed—this is what Paul means to say— it is in actuality confessed that there is a hope that extends beyond death.

Without this hope a Christian cannot persevere. He cannot survive the dangers such as an apostle must constantly accept (vv 30-32), nor does he have a firm footing in this life. Without this hope, one would rather have to say: "Let us eat and drink, for tomorrow we shall die." Here Paul is citing an Old Testament saying (Isa. 22:13), which he takes as a kind of slogan. Without hope that extends beyond death one would have to say that the only sensible thing is to seize whatever sensual pleasure the day affords, as long as the sun shines.

But one should not be deceived! Bad company corrupts

good morals (v 33). Paul cites this statement, which comes from a comedy of the poet Menander, as a familiar saying which was often quoted in that time. He does not add an application. What is meant, however, obviously is that association with people who deny the resurrection of the dead cannot be beneficial to the community in the long run. The results that issue from this will already be easily seen. For thus it is in fact: many members of the church in Corinth must finally awaken from their slumber and become sober; it is high time for this to happen. Some have no awareness of God (v 34). It is likely that this statement contains a polemical note of a special kind. For while the enthusiasts of Corinth boast of possessing the true knowledge of God and of knowing better than anyone else who God is (8:1), Paul confronts them with the charge that they are not even remotely aware of who God is. For through the resurrection of Jesus Christ from the dead God has once for all made known who he is. Anywhere this is not understood, there reigns absolute ignorance, and even the lack of any intimation of God. But that must come to an end. For it is a characteristic of Christians that they are sober and that they declare war on sin.

With this the first train of thought is brought to an end. It is true that in this sequence the apostle has made use in various ways of individual ideas and concepts that made up the eschatological expectation of contemporary Judaism. But the principle that the dead will arise he bases exclusively upon the preaching of the resurrection of Jesus Christ from the dead. Its truth is demonstrated solely in the authoritative power of the proclamation. Wherever it is accepted in faith, there it is understood that the resurrection of Christ is not to be comprehended on the basis of analogies to what can be experienced elsewhere as well, but only as an analogy to what is yet to come.[322] It is true that all human endeavor is moving inevitably toward death. But death will not be the end, because Christ did not remain in the bonds of death. But then the meaning of the Christian faith can never be exhausted in what is presently available; instead, in its very kernel it is the hope and confident expectation of that which indeed is promised, but will only find its fulfillment in the future.[323]

c) The kingdom of God

Against the foregoing affirmations, however, an objection could be raised in which reservations again are registered: "How will the dead be raised?" This question is explained by a second one which is a more precise formulation: "With what kind of body will they come?" (v 35). Herein is expressed the skepticism that had long been current among the Greeks: the body is, after all, perishable and at death will be dissolved into its component parts; only the soul is immortal and can therefore survive death. How then are we to speak of a resurrection of the dead? And how do matters stand with respect to the actuality of the kingdom of God? Paul now enters into discussion with these reflections, first of all by taking up the second statement of the objection and seeking to explain that in fact the resurrection of the dead will be a bodily resurrection. But what does that mean?

In order to explain this, Paul makes use of the figure of the grain of seed. According to the view of that time, the growth through which the plant developed from the seed did not occur simply as a natural process. Instead, first of all the grain of seed must die in the earth, and only then, through a reawakening, is the growth of the plant made possible. Hence in the Gospel of John the figure of seed and growth can be compared with Christ's dying and rising again: "Truly, truly I say to you: unless the grain of wheat falls into the ground and dies, it remains a solitary seed (i e, it produces no fruit). But if it dies (and is reawakened) it produces much fruit." This way—so the application runs—is also destined for Jesus. He must die in order to be raised. For the hour has come when the Son of man will be glorified (John 12:23-24). Thus the grain of seed must first go down into death, in order then to be reawakened and to produce fruit. Only through a divine miracle can there be growth and flourishing (v 36). And how is it then with human life? Paul means to say that it is precisely the same as with seed and fruit (vv 37-38). For in planting it is not the body that will hereafter come forth that is placed in the soil, but a mere grain of seed. God awakens it and gives it a form that did not belong to the seed itself. This idea of an awakening of the seed becomes comprehensible only against the background of the ancient conceptions that Paul shared with his contemporaries. Even though the argument that he employs cannot be appropriated, still the figure that he uses demands that it be understood from the perspective of the specialized expression which is meant to make it vivid: the resurrection of the dead is a resurrection of the whole man, and therefore a bodily resurrection. Nevertheless, it does not come about by means of a continuity that is grounded in man himself, that could survive death. But only the miracle of a divine act produces the resurrection of the dead as a bodily resurrection. Of course this statement requires a more specific explanation.

By way of explanation, the apostle adds a statement by which he calls attention to the fact that in the broad cosmos there are so many different forms of bodies and corporeal phenomena: humans, cattle, birds, fish, and beyond them the sun, moon, and stars. The multiplicity of these creatures, however, is an indication that God, who has made such an abundance of different forms, surely is able in the resurrection of the dead to create something new out of nothing. In saying this, the apostle is thinking of man as a unity that may not be divided into a higher part that is preserved in an immortal soul and a lower part that passes away with the deceased body. Instead, man is, with his body, soul, and spirit, God's creation. The body does not merely cling to him like an outer shell. Rather, since man has a body, he is at the same time body. For this reason Paul can, for example, on the one hand remind the Christians that "*your bodies* are members of Christ" (1 Cor. 6:15), and on the other hand say, "*You* are the body of Christ, and each of you one of his members" (1 Cor. 12:27). "You" has the same meaning in this connection as "your bodies." Man acts through the instrumentality of his body and its members and thereby enters into contact with other persons. This serves to indicate that the whole person is to live as God's creature and to be obedient to the will of his creator—otherwise he would miss his destiny by disregarding God's commandment and falling under slavery to sin. Hence, because human existence is always bodily existence, the resurrection of the dead also will be a bodily resurrection.

After the apostle has pointed to the multiplicity of creaturely beings that exists in the broad cosmos in order to show that God is able at any time to create a new body, he makes the application to the issue that he is treating: "Thus it is with the resurrection of the dead. It is sown perishable and is raised imperishable. It is sown in dishonor and is raised in glory. It is sown in weakness and is raised in strength. It is sown a natural body and is raised a spiritual body" (v 42-44). The contrast is emphasized in four antitheses. Only the miracle of a divine act achieves the resurrection. The point of the train of argument lies in the last statemen: a natural body, which is subject to death and decay, is sown; it is laid in the grave. But God raises up a new body, one that corresponds to the being that is determined by God's Spirit exclusively. If God as the creator made the earthly body, in the resurrection of the dead he will also achieve a new creation. Because God is both creator and Lord, therefore the dead will rise again.

It must be observed that the apostle does not offer any speculations about the form of the new corporeality. In Jewish apocalyptic there was occasionally some reflection on the form and dress of those who would be raised from their tombs. But Paul stops with the statement that the dead will arise and that it will be a bodily resurrection. It is sufficient simply to know this. No conjectures of any sort are offered as to what will be the appearance of an existence hereafter. Anyone who knows that God is God, and that the dead are called into life by him, knows all that it is necessary to know. All else he can commit to God, and he does not need to ask further. Therefore Paul does not continue with any further discussion of the question of how the resurrection of the dead may occur. But he picks up the thread of the preceding statements by referring to the Old Testament once more to demonstrate that the raising of the dead will be a bodily resurrection.

In this train of thought (vv 44b-49) the apostle takes a statement from the creation narrative as his point of departure: man was created as a living being (Gen. 2:7). However, in his doing so, the Old Testament quotation is given a descriptive expansion, in order to be able to append a concluding inference. The words "the first Adam" are inserted, so that the contrast with the "last Adam" results. While the first Adam was created as a "living being," the last Adam became "the Spirit that makes alive." Therewith reference is made once again to the resurrection of Christ from the dead, which in its unique, and at the same time, universal effectiveness is characterized in contrast to Adam. Thus the contrasting of the first and the last man, which in this connection also finds its application (Rom. 5:12-21), here is related to the resurrection of the dead. Thereby the effect that issues from Christ's resurrection to all who belong to him is made clear. The life-creating Spirit, through which Christ's resurrection occurred, also embraces those who belong to Christ and brings about the resurrection from death. While the first man was taken from the earth, the second man came from heaven (v 47).[324] Just as all men who belong to Adam are affected by the fate that issues from him and therefore are earthly, so all those who are on Christ's side will have their destiny determined by him. By way of anticipation, Paul calls them "heavenly," because they are with Christ, who came from heaven. All of us—whether Christians or non-Christians—bear the image of the earthly and belong to Adamic humanity. But we shall bear the image of the heavenly, in that we shall be raised with Christ in glory.

Here end the statements about the question of how the dead are to arise. Although in the process the apostle had adduced quite diverse arguments—the figure of the grain of seed, the multiplicity of creatures in the cosmos, the antithesis of weakness and strength, the understanding of the concept of "body," and a reflection that picks up the thread of the Old Testament—in this train of thought he has steadily maintained that it is appropriate to speak of the resurrection of the dead only in the context of the preaching of Christ. Because Christ has risen from the dead, there is therefore a resurrection of the dead. Christ does not abandon those who are his, but they will be stamped with his image and will bear the image of the heavenly (vv 48-49).

The apostle could have stopped at this point, for he has explained *that* the dead will arise and *how* they will be raised. However, he adds one more brief section, from which it appears that along with his communities, he stood in expectation that Christ's return and the last day would occur in the near future (vv 50-58). The future already extends its reach so immediately into the present that Paul counts on the appearance of Christ in his own lifetime. For this reason he speaks of "us," who will still be alive. But what will happen then? The dead will be awakened and reunited with the community of the living, so that together they might go to meet Christ (1 Thess. 4:13-18). However, in this explanation, what Paul is concerned to show is that no one can enter into the kingdom of God as he is here on earth.

The kingdom of God denotes God's lordship, in which he alone has the rule and everything happens in accordance with his will. With the proclamation of Jesus and the preaching of earliest Christianity Paul is in harmony when he says that the dawning of God's lordship is imminent (Mark 1:15 and par)—so close at hand that its signs are already flashing here and now (Matt. 12-28 and par; Luke 11:28). But who may share in his glory? Flesh and blood—that is, the men who are living here—cannot inherit the kingdom of God (1 Cor. 15:50). While the dead are awakened incorruptible, all who are then alive must be changed from mortality into immortality (v 54). In the kingdom of God there will be no more death. The apostle shares the confident assurance which is also expressed in the last book of the Bible and is described with reference to Isaiah 25:8: Then "God will wipe away all tears from their eyes, and death will be no more, nor will there be any suffering or crying or pain; for the old is passed away. And the one who sat upon the throne said, 'Behold! I make all things new' " (Rev. 21:4-5). In the Corinthian passage Paul not only refers to Isaiah 25:8, but he joins with it a reference to a statement from the book of Hosea (13:14). He combines the two quotations and shapes them into a unitary utterance, which as a jubilant challenge is meant to describe the triumph over death: "Death is swallowed up by victory. Death, where is your victory? Death, where is your sting?" (vv 54-55). At the end, death falls into the maelstrom of the perishing world and with it is destined for defeat.

Paul appends to this section a brief comment which takes up the word "sting" and concisely indicates the context that is crucial for his theological thinking. "But the sting of death is sin, and the strength of sin is the law" (v 56). In the statements of 1 Corinthians 15, the justification of the sinner was not explicitly the theme under discussion. This idea was constantly in the apostle's mind, however, as is shown at the end by this reference. The sting with which death oppresses man is the power of sin. But it has established its dominion with the help of the Law. This connection is traced out by Paul more explicitly in the Epistle to the Romans (6:23; 7:7-25); here he only alludes to it. While in Romans, Paul explains the doctrine of justification by pointing to the fact that God awakens the dead and calls into being the things that are not (Rom. 4:17), in the present passage he connects the resurrection of the dead with the doctrine of justification. In both passages what is involved is the same kind of divine action. God justifies the ungodly, and he awakens the dead. Not in us, but only in him is there righteousness, which he bestows upon those who trust in his word. Not in us, but only in him is life, which he produces by creation, so that even death must admit defeat, give up the fight, and lay down its arms. Therefore Paul cannot but conclude his statements with jubilant thanksgiving, "Thanks be to God, who gives us the victory through our Lord Jesus Christ" (v 57). God gives this victory even now; even now the song of jubilation can begin. But it follows from this that Christians have to meet the tasks of their life soberly, steadfastly, and unshakably, sustained by the confidence that their work is not in vain in the Lord (v 58). Because the Christians' activity is marked by hope, it is the expression of grateful response to the gospel which proclaims Christ's resurrection as the beginning and the earnest-money of the resurrection of the dead.[325]

In the debate with the Corinthians the apostle Paul showed that he understood the existence of the believers as the life of those who are marked by the belief in Christ's resurrection and the hope of their own resurrection. But if this belief and this hope cannot be grounded solely on profound thoughts which one can cherish alongside other serious reflections, it is also true that they cannot represent mere ornamentation or edifying consolation, but they must fill the whole being of the Christian. Where this belief and this hope are maintained, everything that is said about man therefore must stand under this superscription: resurrection of the dead.[326]

I. The new life in Christ

a) Eternal life

What is meant when one speaks of eternal life? This question is treated with special intensity in the Gospel of John. There the gift of eternal life is not understood as a blessing of the hereafter, but as the reality that encounters faith already, here and now. Thus the Johannine Christ says, "Truly, truly, I say to you, whoever hears my word and believes him who sent me has eternal life and does not come into judgment, but has passed from death to life" (John 5:24). In this declaration, which is introduced with a solemn assurance, the traditional concepts of eschatological expectation are employed. It speaks of hearing and believing, of life, death, and judgment. What is thought of here, however, is not a future event that will occur at the end of history. There is no description of the judgment that will be held for all men at the last day. Instead, this states what happens when a person accepts Jesus' word, heeding it, and is receptive to him in faith. That person recognizes in Jesus the one whom the Father has sent into the world as savior. Anyone who turns to him, trusting, and gives heed to his word has thereby taken the step by which everything is to be decided, and indeed is already decided. For that person is now delivered from judgment. No longer can any sentence be pronounced against him, and no one can condemn him.

Anyone who believes in Jesus as God's Son is not judged. But conversely, "Whoever does not believe is already judged, because he does not believe in the name of the only Son of God" (John 3:18). This means that the definitive judgment already occurs where a person refuses the love of God that comes to him in Christ. But faith comprehends that Christ has opened up to him eternal life. This life does not begin only after physical death and does not first unfold in a celestial world. Instead, eternal life is life that truly merits this name: to be in fellowship with God, to belong to him so firmly that neither pain nor

affliction, neither death nor decay, can separate one from him.
For one whom God has addressed, and who has responded to
him affirmatively, is therewith affected by his creative word
that works to achieve and fulfill what it declares. Therewith,
however, through the transformation of the present moment
into eternal life, a future is opened up which no power on earth,
neither devil nor death, can bring to an end. For eternal life is
God's life, true life in contradistinction to all life that is
transient, that is unceasingly subject to decay and dissolution.
For this reason it is said that whoever believes this has already
passed from death to life and will not come into judgment.

Eternal life cannot be displayed, so that anyone and
everyone could scrutinize it in order then to consider whether
he should undertake to gain it with this offer or should reject it.
Instead, this offer is encountered only in the proffered word of
Jesus Christ, to which faith responds. For, as the Johannine
Christ says, this is "eternal life, to acknowledge that thou art the
only true God and that Jesus Christ is the one whom thou hast
sent (John 17:3). Hence to believe means to receive the real life.
Utilizing concepts that were current elsewhere, in which the
eschatological expectation was expressed, this idea is expressed
thus: "Truly, truly, I say to you, the hour is coming, and indeed
is already here, when the dead will hear the voice of the Son of
God, and all who hear it will live" (John 5:25). Here the
resurrection of the dead is spoken of as it is described in
apocalyptic images by Jews and Christians alike. However, it is
not identified as an event that is still awaited, that may occur in
the more immediate or the more distant future. Instead, the
resurrection of the dead is already occurring here and now. For
whoever accepts the call of Jesus Christ hears the voice of the
Son of man that calls forth the dead from their graves. He
belongs to the company of those who are of the truth and
recognize the truth. For this is identified as the aim of the
mission and the work of Jesus: "For this reason I was born and
came into the world, to bear witness to the truth. Whoever is of
the truth will hear my voice" (John 18:37).

The biblical concept of truth denotes that which is
unconditionally valid and is so trustworthy that one can rely on
it at all times. The truth is certain; one can build on it, come

what may. Hence it is said of God that he is the guardian of truth, in whose word one can place unconditional confidence. His ways are just, so that one can proceed in them with sure step. This truth is not gained as a result of human inquiry, searching, and meditation, at which one finally arrives after careful consideration of arguments and counterarguments. Instead, because it is God's truth, it always precedes men, and is disclosed to them as that which God has established and now bestows upon them as the firm and secure footing of their life. Anyone who has comprehended that the truth is given to man by God understands how this world is created in truth, and therewith he acquires the capacity for acting rationally and responsibly. According to the original meaning of the Greek word, truth is "the manifest," that which is exhibited in unveiled clarity and without ambiguity. This manifest truth, however, is exclusively God's doing, and man can have an intimation of it and comprehend it only where he is encountered by something that transcends his sphere of experience, where he is struck and seized by that which supports him as the very basis and ground of his life. Jesus bore witness to this truth, which is given as the answer to all human searching and inquiring. Indeed more: this truth is nothing other than Jesus himself (John 14:6). In him the seeking and searching of men finds the only valid answer. Hence, whoever is of the truth, whoever feels the impact of the Word of truth which is Jesus himself, perceives this his voice as the Word of truth.

In the light of this truth, which is Jesus Christ, it is made manifest what is the situation in which this world actually exists. Because Jesus is the truth, it therefore becomes evident that without him people live in untruth. Because Jesus is the life, it therefore is manifest that without him all are in death. For the way of every man ends in death, in nothingness, in utter decay. But at the end of all ways there stands, not perdition, but Christ as the truth and the life. Through the truth that is Jesus of Nazareth, God himself has intervened in the untruth, the falsehood, and the darkness of the world, to overcome them and to open up the way of the truth. But this way of the truth is traveled in love. For the faith that has heard Jesus' voice awakens the power of love. Hence it can be said in 1 John (3:14), "We know that we have passed from death to life, because we love the brethren. Anyone who does not love abides in death."

Apparently these statements were already very early felt to be too strong, so that they were expanded by means of additions, to conform to the traditional perspective on the hope that was future-oriented, and were thereby significantly restricted. An editor who revised the original text of the Gospel of John therefore inserted the verses: "For the hour is coming when all who are in their graves will hear his voice, and those who have done good will come forth to the resurrection of life, but those who have done evil will come forth to the resurrection of judgment" (5:28-29).[327] Here the gaze is turned once again toward the last day that will sometime appear. Then the great division between men will take place, so that the wicked will be separated from the righteous. The resurrection of life is set in contrast to a resurrection of judgment, which leads to the irrevocable pronouncement of a final and definitive verdict. But in contrast to this editorial expansion, the evangelist John places all his emphasis upon the declaration that faith has already passed through the judgment, and has made the transition out of death into the life that no death is any longer able to disturb or destroy.

Believest thou this?—the preaching of the evangelist focuses upon this question. It is expounded in the conversation which Martha, the sister of the deceased Lazarus, and Jesus had at the tomb of the departed one (John 11:20-27). Martha addresses Jesus with the remark that if he had been there, her brother would not have died. Yet, in spite of this disappointment, which she cannot conceal, she expresses the conviction that, whatever Jesus would ask of God, God would grant it to him. Thereupon Jesus says to her that her brother will rise again. But what does this mean? Martha understands this declaration in the sense of the traditional expectation that is connected with the resurrection of the dead at the last day. Hence, she expresses in correct formulation the assurance that was shared by large segments of the Judaism of that time. "I know that he will rise—at the resurrection on the last day" (11:24). But can such an expectation signify the fulfillment of the hope that death might weaken and life prevail? It is oriented to a future that is still awaited, and it does not take into consideration the possibility that God could act here and now.

Jesus allows Martha's answer to stand, without refuting it. But the word that he now addresses to her takes an entirely new direction and draws the concepts of resurrection and life out of the future into the present. "I am the resurrection and the life" (John 11:25). This statement must be seen in connection with the other "I am" sayings in the Gospel of John: bread of life, light of the world, the door, the good shepherd, the true vine.[328] Each of these concepts denotes the goal of men's hopes. For every man would like to be satisfied and yet at the same time knows that he cannot live by bread alone. Every man needs light in order to be able to live and strives toward the light that will finally drive out the darkness. Every man knows that he must die, and longs for life that might not be subject to decay and dissolution. Reference is made to these expectations in the words of the Johannine Christ, in order to say: The bread of life, of which all know how desperately they need it—here it is. The light of the world, without which the world must perish in the shadow of darkness—here it shines. Resurrection and life, which alone will bring about the destruction of death—here they are. Here the form in which these statements are cast is reminiscent of a style of discourse that is prefigured in the Old Testament. Thus the prophet asks, "Who has performed and done this, calling the generations from the beginning?" And the answer is: "I, the Lord, the first, and with the last; I am He" (Isa. 41:4 RSV). In answer to the question as to where then is to be found the one who is able to bring the hopes to realization, it is said: Here is the one; I am He. With this word the God of Israel is represented as the one who is infinitely superior to the gods of the Gentiles.

But then it is clear what the Johannine sayings of Christ are declaring. They point to the expectation that is shared by all men, and they emphasize that this expectation is fulfilled in Christ—in him alone. Bread of life—light of the world—resurrection and life: it is Christ, no one and nothing else besides him. In this affirmation, there is a statement about what he is for those who believe in him, and what he does for them.

Therefore, as a rule there is a further statement appended to the "I am" saying, providing a more explicit interpretation. "I am the bread of life; whoever comes to me will never more hunger, and whoever believes on me will never thirst again" (6:35). "I am the light of the world; anyone who follows after me will not remain in darkness, but will have the light of life" (8:12). And so here also: "I am the resurrection and the life; he who believes in me, though he die, yet shall he live, and whoever lives and believes in me shall never die" (11:25-26 RSV). This means that the resurrection and the life are not bestowed apart from Christ, but only in such a way that he is believed and received as the resurrection and the life. Thus, what Jesus promises to men is not this or that gift, but himself. Life and death are not states of being that exist in isolation from him. But he alone is life in the true sense.[329] This gift, which he both is and bestows, is not found in heaven or in some distant future, but it is bestowed through him to those who belong to him. For—as Martin Luther comments on this expression in the Gospel of John—"the one on whom you believe is not in heaven and the resurrection here on earth. You shall not separate me from the resurrection and the life."[330]

In an utterance that is given a parallel construction, it is explained in positive and negative terms what resurrection and life mean for those who trust in Christ; and in this process, there is an exposition of the reciprocal connection between believing, living, and dying. Anyone who believes in Christ as the resurrection and the life will live, even though he must die an earthly death. And conversely: anyone who lives and believes in him will never die. It is true that this person remains subject to physical death and must suffer it. But the power of life that Christ is and gives cannot be destroyed even by death. For death has lost the character of finality for the person who belongs to Christ. It is true that suffering, pain, and woe are not thereby abolished, but the terror is taken out of death. The life that Jesus Christ is and bestows, however, is distinguished from the life of all men by the fact that their life leads inexorably toward death, while the life of Jesus Christ comes out of death. For he has been raised from the dead to the life that no death can now destroy. Inasmuch as Jesus Christ has given to those

who believe in him and belong to him a share in this his life,
they too have death behind them, even though they yet must
die. But the physical death that still awaits them now is so
sharply distinguished from the death to which all life otherwise
is subjected that it can no longer offer any real competition to
life. [331]

"Believest thou this?" asks Jesus. He does not ask whether
Martha has comprehended what she has heard, or whether she
was able to follow him with her understanding. For it is only in
faith that one can understand the whole issue here. Martha
expresses this faith by taking up and repeating words of
confession: "Yes, Lord, I believe that you are the Christ, the
Son of God, who has come into the world" (11:27). With these
words she acknowledges that in him, God's activity has broken
into the world, and through that activity, victory over death has
been given to life. Even though in all areas of their lives men are
surrounded and threatened by death, still the Christian can,
and indeed must, say with Martin Luther: "Life is concealed
behind death. The reason does not comprehend this, but faith
says, 'I die into Christ; wherever I may go, I shall find him
there. . . . Therefore for me death is better than life. . . . Thus
I see life in death.' "[332]

b) Dying and rising with Christ

Christ's dying and rising again have wrought a fundamental change in the relationship of life and death for all who belong
to him. According to the conviction of earliest Christianity, all
those who are baptized into Christ are incorporated into his
dying and rising again. The apostle Paul reminds the church at
Rome of this knowledge, which is common to all Christians, and
declares: "All of us who were baptized into Christ Jesus were
baptized into his death" (Rom. 6:3). In these words he uses a
manner of expression that was altogether common in the
hellenistic environment of the primitive Christian communities.

In the communities of the mystery religions, cultic initiatory actions were performed, through which the initiates were supposed to be united with the fate of a cultic deity. In most cases this involved deities that were originally worshiped in the Orient, but then had found followers throughout the entire Mediterranean area. The cult's myth told of their dying and rising again, and therewith described the coming-into-being and the passing-away that are constantly going on in nature. People of the ancient world were moved by the strong yearning to be filled with divine power, in order thereby to receive life that will survive death and will lift one above the manifold disappointments and sufferings of this world. Such power was promised by the mystery religions to their adherents. It was supposed to be imparted, through the initiation, to everyone who placed himself in the service of a deity and paid homage to that deity. Silence was to be maintained concerning the religious ceremony, lest the mystery be profaned. Yet in more or less clear intimations, variously given by ancient authors, it is reported how an initiate was led into dark underground chambers, clothed at the initiation in new robes, and then brought up again to the light. In this way he was incorporated into the dying and rising, and thus into the fate of the cultic deity, so that the vital powers that issue from the deity might flow through him and deify him. "I went"—so one initiate relates—"to the very boundary between life and death. I crossed the threshold of Proserpina.[333] And after I had passed through all the elements, I returned once again. At the very hour of midnight I saw the sun shining with its bright light; I beheld the lower and the higher gods face to face, and I worshiped them in their presence."[334]

Even though the Christians of the hellenistic communities made use of this manner of expression and applied it to baptism, still they gave a new meaning to these words. For they were not speaking of an initiatory ceremony that dispenses divine powers and immortality to the initiates. Instead, they were saying that the person who is baptized is incorporated into the death and resurrection of Jesus Christ. But in what way is he connected with this occurrence? Paul speaks with the primitive Christian communities of undergoing an actual death: "We are buried with him by baptism into death" (Rom. 6:4). The reference to a tomb emphasizes the fact that a life actually has ended. By this the apostle means the old life in which we were subject to the power of sin, so that we had to serve it as slaves. But now through death all legal obligations are cancelled, and the bonds are once and for all dissolved. However, while in the thought of the mystery religions people spoke not only of a dying, but also of an already accomplished resurrection in the sense of a filling with divine power as the gift of immortality, Paul gives to this train of ideas an entirely different direction. That is, he completes the sentence with the following words: "so that as Christ was raised from the dead by the glory of the Father, we also might walk in a new life" (Rom. 6:4). That is to say, death has already occurred, but the resurrection still lies before us. However, the future event of the resurrection of the dead is intended to, and should, determine the life of those who are baptized into Christ, who are stamped with his name and believe on him.[335] Through baptism the Christian is committed to his Lord, so that in faith he grasps the gift of new life which from this point onward guides and sustains his thinking, speaking, and acting.

Paul explains this idea by repeating it, using different concepts. "Our old man has been crucified with him" (Rom.6:6). Here he is looking back at the past and saying that it has been nailed to the cross with Christ, so that it has definitively come to an end. "We have died with Christ" (Rom. 6:8). This sharp line of separation not only has once and for all put an end to the past; it also identifies the new beginning, which now functions in an obligatory way: We belong to Christ, and hence we stand on the side of life, not of death—on the side of a new behavior, not of submission to sin. But from this assurance there follows the confidence that "we believe that we shall also live with him" (Rom. 6:8).

The Epistle to the Colossians, which was written by a pupil of the apostle, goes beyond these Pauline utterances. For it speaks not only of a death that one undergoes in baptism, but also of a resurrection that has already occurred in baptism as well:[336] "You were buried with him by baptism, and with him you were also raised, through faith in the power of God, who raised him from the dead" (Col. 2:12). In contrast to Romans 6, the emphasis now is placed upon the declaration: you have been raised with him; in baptism the resurrection already has actually occurred. Nevertheless, in saying this, the Epistle to the Colossians is far from falling victim to a frenzy of fanaticism or thinking of the bestowal of immortality, such as was imagined in the communities of the mystery religions. Instead, to be raised with Christ means nothing other than to have the forgiveness of sins and therefore to lead a new life. For—so the passage continues—to this end "God made you alive with him, you who were dead in sins" (2:13). Therewith the old life is simply characterized as a death, in which one was formerly held captive. But from this death God has called forth and awakened to new life all who have been baptized into Christ and who believe in him.

Whoever has experienced this has to draw the necessary conclusion. "If you are risen with Christ, seek the things that are above, where Christ is, seated at the right hand of God. Set your mind on the things that are above, not on the things that are on the earth. For you have died, and your life is hid with Christ in God. But when Christ, your life, shall appear, then you also will appear with him in glory" (Col. 3:1-4). This summons is simply filled with a hymnic tone. God's deed has already happened. He has already called us out of death into life. This life, of course, is not transposed, as divine fullness and power, into immortality. But the summons to believing fulfillment is derived from the coming of salvation that has already occurred: "Seek the things that are above." Thus the goal is held up before the eyes of such seeking and striving. To look toward the things that are above means to turn one's gaze to where Christ is with God. Therefore even in the midst of this world, those who are his are already connected with the heavenly world. For he who is the head is above, and those who belong to him cling steadfastly to him, knowing that they are liberated from all that would drag them down. Therewith the direction is indicated for the way of the Christians, in which they must turn their steps.

That which once prevailed no longer holds true. The old life is once and for all abolished by the death which has been suffered with Christ. Yet the new life that is imparted by God's creative power is a reality only where it is accepted and lived "by faith" (Col. 2:12). This means a decisive rejection of the fanatical conception that salvation is already visibly present in unbroken fullness, death has already disappeared, and the resurrection of the dead has already occurred. The old life has ended with the death which has been suffered with Christ, so that the past can no longer make any claim upon the believer. But the life which God has created in the resurrection with Christ is and remains utterly bound to Christ, and therefore it is not placed at the disposal of man. Man has this life only where he lives with Christ and trusts his Lord. But because the life of those who have risen with Christ still is withheld from the view of men and is hidden from them, they need the admonition by which they are strengthened in their holding fast to the gospel and are urged to demonstrate that life in their conduct. In this connection, the spatial distinction between "above" and "below" serves to illustrate the either-or character of the decision which defines the life of the Christian. This decision has already been made, with binding force, in the dying and rising with Christ. Therefore, in the actions of the believers it is requisite to put off the old man, which has died with Christ, and to put on the new man, which God has created and has called into life in the resurrection with Christ (Col. 3:5-17).

c) The Christian's living and dying

The apostle Paul says of the conduct of Christians that the death of the old life lies behind them, for they are crucified with Christ (Gal. 2:19). Those who belong to Christ have crucified the flesh together with all its passions and lusts (Gal. 5:24). They have renounced their own will, in which their desires and their striving served as the standard for all their thinking and acting. Instead, in faith they have taken upon themselves the cross of Christ as their cross and thereby have set out upon a new way. "Now I no longer live, but Christ lives in me. But so long as I live in this body, I live in faith in the Son of God, who loved me and gave himself for me" (Gal. 2:20). The apostle does not forget

that he is still on this earth, experiences the joy and the burden
of physical existence, and at the last must die. He is fully aware
that he continues to be subject to the conditions and the
possibilities of human existence, as all other men are. But a
change has come about in his life, which has changed and
renewed everything, from the ground up. Because he has been
effectively brought into association with the dying and rising of
Jesus Christ, henceforth this participation fills his entire life.
He looks back upon the death which he has experienced with
Christ, and therefore sees only life before him. It is true that
one day he will have to die, as it is required of all men. But all
the days that lie before him now stand under the banner of the
life that has been bestowed upon him with Christ. This life is so
wholly bound to Christ and so indissolubly linked with his name
that it cannot be described in any other way than by saying that
now Christ lives in him, and therefore Christ is his life. Now, as
Martin Luther says, there is no longer any "I" that could be
separated or distinguished from Christ. That "I" that was
without him and that thought it could live without him, belongs
rather to death and hell. "But now Christ abides in me, and this
life exists in me. Hence the life that I now live is Christ."[337]

Thus Paul views everything that can happen to the
Christian in the context of this certainty, so that no one lives to
himself and no one dies to himself, but "If we live, we live unto
the Lord; and if we die, we die unto the Lord. Therefore,
whether we live or die, we belong to the Lord. For it is for this
purpose that Christ died and lived again, that he might be Lord
of the dead and of the living" (Rom. 14:8-9). Man's relationship
to God is no longer dependent on whether he lives or dies.
Instead, it is determined solely by Jesus Christ and by the faith
that trusts him, in living and in dying.

The Christian can accept every day that is given to him as a
gift of God and can put his hand to the tasks that are set before
him as a commission from God. He has no reason inwardly to
detach himself from the world and prematurely to bid farewell
to the world. Just as he places life and death in the hands of his
Lord, and receives them from him, so also he accepts with
grateful heart what God's creation provides and bestows. He
has learned from his Lord not to be consumed with anxious

thoughts about the future, or about food and clothing. Nevertheless, he also will not despise the world or lightly esteem it, but will conduct his life in the confident assurance that as a creature of God he can trust his Lord in all his ways, and therefore in comforted confidence can joyfully make his way.

To be sure, it would be a delusion to think that this new life of the Christians is freed from cares and sufferings. On the contrary, Christians are incorporated not only into the life of Christ, but also into his sufferings, and therefore they understand that they cannot go their way other than in readiness to submit to persecution and pain for Christ's sake, in patience. Paul reminds the churches that his apostolic ministry must be performed under extraordinary burdens. "To the present hour we hunger and thirst, we are ill-clad and buffeted and homeless" (1 Cor. 4:11 RSV). It must be this way, because he and his co-laborers in the persecution bear in their bodies the dying of Jesus (2 Cor. 4:10). But precisely therein they have the marvelous experience of learning that they do not perish, but the life of Jesus becomes manifest in their mortal bodies. "For in the midst of life we are always being given over to death for Jesus' sake, so that the life of Jesus also might be made manifest in our mortal bodies" (2 Cor. 4:11). If Christ was crucified in weakness, then the person who follows him cannot expect his life to be marked by signs and evidences of strength and power. But as Christ was crucified in weakness, but lives by the power of God, so also those who are his will be weak in him, but with him will live by the power of God (2 Cor. 13:4). If God's power is at work precisely where there is nothing, then to those who become conscious of their weakness and helplessness, God's strength is imparted: "with great endurance, in sufferings, in afflictions, in calamities, in beatings, in imprisonments, in persecutions, in toils, in watching . . . as unknown, and yet well known; as dying, and behold, we live; as punished, and yet not killed; as sorrowful, but always joyous; as poor, but yet making many rich; as those who have nothing, and yet have everything" (2 Cor. 6:4-5, 9-10). In this, the gaze of the Christian is directed forward; for he wants "to know him and the power of his resurrection and the fellowship of his sufferings, and thus to become conformed to his death," so that he might attain to the resurrection of the dead (Phil. 3:10-11).

Paul does not share the perspective of the Stoic philosophers, who are inwardly fortified completely against feeling any pain, grief, or anxiety, so that nothing of that sort can anymore reach them, because it does not concern their true "I". But the apostle regards everything that happens to him in his life in the light of the new life that is given to him by and through Christ. For this reason he is able to view with an incomparable inward tranquillity and freedom everything that happens around him and that could throw him into a state of grave anxiety. In prison he writes to the church at Philippi and tells them that his situation is so serious that he must reckon with the possibility that the proceedings that are being pressed against him will end with his death. Nevertheless, his words sound the note of joy, and he exhorts his readers to rejoice in the Lord always. For himself, he hopes nothing other than that Christ may be glorified in his body, "whether by life or by death" (Phil. 1:20).

The apostle is ready to travel the way that God has determined for him. He says that Christ is his life, and dying will be gain. In this situation, he does not know which he would prefer. On the one hand, he feels the desire to depart from the world and to be with Christ. On the other hand, he is aware that the churches need him, and he must remain with them (Phil. 1:21-26). When Paul says, "I long to depart and to be with Christ" (1:23), he does not devote a single word to a description of the coming glory, but characterizes it only with the name of Christ. But the same name also stands for life and for the task that Paul has to fulfill here. Therefore, it can come however it may; in any case Christ will be determinative for his living and his dying. Thus Paul is not inclined to the attitude of wishing to bid farewell to the world, weary and resigned. Instead, he places himself wholly in the hands of his Lord, to whom he lives and dies.[338]

Whatever happens, the Christian is sustained by the certainty that "neither death nor life, neither angels nor powers, nor principalities, neither present nor future, neither height nor depth, nor any other creature can separate us from the love of God which is in Christ Jesus our lord" (Rom. 8:38-39). The utterances from the Epistle to the Romans give voice to a song of triumph whose notes appear almost too lofty to be grasped. In this passage, the apostle makes use of hymnic expressions to describe the immeasurable strength that God bestows upon those who set their hopes, not in their own capacities, but in the one who raises the dead. Could it ever come to the point—this is the question—that the love which God has given to us in Christ would end? The Christian is able to imagine all sorts of situations. He can be seized by anxiety, or he can make his way into a blind alley that apparently has no exit. He can be maligned or persecuted. Indeed, it can happen that he becomes weak and unsure in faith. External dangers can threaten him and block his way. Hostile forces and powers can shake his life, so that he thinks he has been abandoned to a blind fate. It can appear that the stars guide the course of all events. But they still remain God's creatures, which he has made and which have to serve him. Neither they nor any event that could intrude upon one's life will be able to erect a dividing wall that could keep God's love at a distance. On the contrary, there is no one so powerful that he could frustrate God's purpose—not even death, that stands at the end of all roads. God's love, which did not leave Christ in death, but raised him from the dead, is stronger than all else that could be, in heaven and on earth.

The assured confidence that grows out of this certainty is able to stand the test of the bitter reality of death. This has been demonstrated in the dying hours of many. Thus, the friends of Martin Luther who were with him at his end relate that he uttered a final prayer, in which he said: "O my heavenly Father, the one God and Father of our Lord Jesus Christ, thou God of all comfort, I thank thee that thou hast revealed to me thy dear Son Jesus Christ, in whom I believe, whom I have preached and confessed, whom I have loved and adored. I beseech thee, my Lord Jesus Christ, let my soul be commended to thee. O heavenly Father, though I must now leave this body and be taken from this life, still I know with assurance that I shall abide with thee eternally, and no one can pluck me out of thy hands."[339]

Notes

1. On this topic cf J. Reese, *Hellenistic Influence on the Book of Wisdom and Its Consequences*, Analecta Biblica (AnBib) 41 (Rome, 1970), pp 33-34 and 146 ff. On the concept of the Apocrypha, cf L. Rost, *Judaism Outside the Hebrew Canon: An Introduction to the Documents*, David E. Green, tr. (Nashville 1976), pp 21 ff; 25 ff; and below, pp 54 ff.—On the literary problems connected with the Wisdom of Solomon, cf Rost, pp 56 ff.

2. Life of Adam and Eve 12 ff, in *The Apocrypha and Pseudepigrapha of the Old Testament (APOT)*, R. H. Charles, ed. (Oxford, 1913), II, pp 137 ff, and Apocalypse of Moses 15 ff, in *APOT II*, pp 147 ff. On the literary problem connected with the Life of Adam and Eve, cf Rost, pp 151 ff.

3. On this matter, cf below, pp 68 ff.

4. His spiritual and intellectual kinship to Enoch 1–36 and 91-107 has been emphasized by P. Grelot, "L'eschatologie de la Sagesse et les apocalypses juives," in *A la rencontre de Dieu. Mémorial A. Gelin* (Lyons, 1961), pp 173 ff.

5. On this topic, cf Reese (above, n 1), pp 160 ff, and Grelot (above, n 4), pp 165 ff.

6. Cf F. Gogarten, "Die christliche Hoffnung," *Deutsche Universitätszeitung 9*, 24 (1954), pp 3 ff.

7. Plato, *Phaedo* 69E–70A.

8. *Phaedo* 70E; cf 76A.

9. *Phaedo* 114C. On this matter cf E. Ehmark, "Transmigration in Plato," *Harvard Theological Review* (HTR) 50 (1957), pp 1 ff, and P. Friedländer, *Platon* (Berlin, 3rd ed, 1964), I, pp 182 ff, and especially pp 191 ff. A brief overview of the Greek belief in the hereafter is provided by W. Jaeger, "The Greek Ideas of Immortality," HTR 52 (1959), pp 135 ff; also published in *Immortality and Resurrection*, Krister Stendahl, ed. (New York, 1965), pp 97 ff.

10. *Gorgias* 473A; cf 469B and 527.

11 *Phaedrus* 245C 246A.

12. On this point cf K. Rahner, *Foundations of Christian Faith. An Introduction to the Idea of Christianity*, William V. Dych, tr. (New York, 1978), pp 75 ff.

13. On this point cf Rahner (above, n 12), pp 264 ff, and especially p 268.

14. Cf. Cicero, *Tusculan Disputations* I, 31 and 36, but also the reappropriation of the concept by C. G. Jung, *The Structure and Dynamics of the Psyche*, R. F. C. Hull, tr. Vol. 8 of *The Collected Works of C. G. Jung*, Bollingen Series XX (New York, 1960), pp 404 ff.

15. On this point cf G. von Rad, *Genesis: A Commentary*, John H. Marks, tr. (Philadelphia, revised edition, 1972), pp 57 ff, and W. Zimmerli, *Old Testament Theology in Outline*, David E. Green, tr. (Atlanta, 1978), pp 35 ff.

16. Cf also Enoch 25:6, and on this passage, below, p 84.

17. On the problem of the literary growth of the saying, which is evident even in the translation of this passage, cf, e g, von Rad, pp 94-95.

18. Thus also von Rad (above, n 15), pp 95-96.

19 Cf R. Martin-Achard, "De la mort à la résurrection," Bibliothèque de

théologie. 3rd. series. Théologie biblique (BT.B) (Paris and Neuchatel, 1956), pp 23-24 and 45, as well as von Rad, *op cit.*

20. On this point cf K. Budde, *Die biblische Paradiesgeschichte,* Beihefte zur Zeitschrift für die Alttestamentliche Wissenschaft (BZAW) 60 (Giessen, 1932), pp 16 ff.

21. Cf O. H. Steck, *Die Paradieserzählung,* Biblische Studien (BSt) 60 (Neukirchen, 1970), pp 116 ff.

22. Cf the translations in *Altorientalische Texte zum Alten Testament* (AOT), 2nd ed., pp 143 ff, and *Ancient Near Eastern Tests Relating to the Old Testament (ANET),* James B. Pritchard, ed. (Princeton, 2nd ed., corrected and enlarged, 1955), pp 101 ff. On this matter, cf also O. Weber, *Die Literatur der Babylonier und Assyrer* (Leipzig, 1907), pp 105 ff, and F. M. Th. de Liagre Böhl, "Die Mythe vom weisen Adapa," *Welt des Orients* (WO) 2, 5/6 (1959), pp 416 ff.

23. Cf the Greek myth of the apples of the Hesperides, discussed in H. J. Rose, *A Handbook of Greek Mythology* (London, 5th ed., 1953), p 23, and the selections from sources and the illustrations in F. Brommer, *Herakles. Die zwölf Taten des Helden in antiker Kunst und Literatur* (Darmstadt, 1972), pp 47 ff. Cf further the mythological idea of nectar and ambrosia as the magical nourishment of the gods, and on this see the *Odyssey* V.196 ff. and V.85 ff. On the tree of life, cf also E. O. James, *The Tree of life. An Archaeological Study,* Studies in the History of Religions (SHR) 11 (Leiden, 1966).

24. On the *Gilgamesh Epic,* cf A. L. Oppenheim, *Ancient Mesopotamia* (Chicago, 1964), pp 255 ff; F. M. Th. de Liagre Böhl, "Das Problem ewigen Lebens im Zyklus und Epos des Gilgamesch," in *Opera Minora* (Groningen and Djakarta, 1973), pp 234 ff. Translations are given in *AOT,* pp 150 ff, and *ANET,* pp 72 ff, as well as in *The Epic of Gilgamesh. An English Version with an Introduction,* by N. K. Sandars (Harmondsworth, Middlesex, 1960, 1964).

25. The sun-god. On the Mesopotamian deities, cf the pertinent articles by O. E. Edzard in the *Wörterbuch der Mythologie* I, H. W. Haussig, ed. (Stuttgart, 1965).

26. *Gilgamesh Epic,* Tablet III.IV.5 ff.

27. *Gilgamesh Epic,* Tablet X.II.1 ff.

28. On this point cf E. F. Wente, "Egyptian 'Make Merry' Songs Reconsidered," *Journal of Near Eastern Studies* (JNES) 21 (1967), pp 118 ff, and H. Brunner, "Wiederum die ägyptischen 'Make Merry' Lieder," *JNES* 25 (1966), pp 130 ff, which demonstrate that the harpists' songs originally did not possess a funerary character, but were sung at secular festivals and other occasions. Cf also the harpists' songs in S. Schott, *Altägyptische Liebeslieder,* Bibliothek der Alten Welt (Zurich, 1950), pp 54-55.

29. Cf Ecclesiastes 5:9-19; 8:9-15; 8:16–9:10; 11:7–12:6.

30. Cf, e. g., Mimnermus, fr. 2 (Diehl), tr. in H. Fränkel, *Dichtung und Philosophie des frühen Griechentums* (Munich, 3rd ed. 1969), p 241; Alcaeus, fr. 20 (D); 73 (D); 91 (D), Greek and German in M. Treu, *Alkaios,* Tusculum-Bücherei (Munich, 2nd ed. 1963).

31. *Carmina* I.11.8; cf II.3, II.14, and II.18. On the ancient understanding of death, cf also M. Roncelaar, "Das Leben mit dem Tode in der Antike," in *Grenzerfahrung Tod,* A. Paus, ed. (Graz-Vienna-Cologne, 1976), pp 83 ff.

32. *Gilgamesh Epic,* Tablet X.III.1 ff, in Sandars, p 99.

33. The storm-god.

34. Since the work of L. Malten, "Elysion und Rhadamanthys," *Jahrbuch des deutschen archäologischen Instituts (JDAI)* 28 (1913), p 35, the Cretan

mediation of the idea of Elysium has been regarded as proven. Cf, e g, F. Schachermeyr, *Die minoische Kultur des alten Kreta* (Stuttgart, 1964), p 305.

35. Hesiod, *Works and Days* 166 ff; cf Pindar, *Olympian Odes* 2.68 ff.

36. Cf Erwin Rohde, *Psyche. The Cult of Souls and Belief in Immortality among the Greeks*, W. B. Hillis, tr. (London, 1925), pp 55 ff.

37. On this point, cf below, p. 28.

38. As a parallel, cf what the hellenized Babylonian priest Berossos tells about the transporting of the hero of the deluge, Xisuthros, in *AOT*, p 201.

39. On the Ethiopic Book of Enoch, cf Rost (above, n 1), pp 133 ff, and now by all means J. T. Milik, *The Books of Enoch. Aramaic Fragments of Qumran Cave 4* (Oxford, 1976), pp 4 ff, and esp pp 22 ff.

40. On the book of Jubilees, cf Rost (above, n 1), pp 129 ff.

41. On this point cf H.-Chr. Schmitt, *Elisa* (Gütersloh, 1972), pp 102 ff.

42. On this point cf Deut. 33:26; Ps. 18:10; 68:4, 33; 104:3; Isa. 19:1; and Hab. 3:8. On the cherubim as personified storm-clouds, cf W. Eichrodt, *Theology of the Old Testament*, J. A. Baker, tr. (Philadelphia, 1967), Vol. 2, pp 203-4, and E. Würthwein, *Die Bücher der Könige*, Das Alte Testament Deutsch (ATD) 11.1 (Göttingen, 1977), p 67.

43. On this point cf R. Hillmann, *Wasser und Berg* (Dissertation, Halle, 1965), pp 14 ff, and C. Houtman, *De Hemel in het Oude Testament* (Franeker, 1974), pp 74-75.

44. Cf also below, pp. 29.

45. On the problem of the literary connection beween the two stories, cf Schmitt, *Elisa*, pp 153-54; on the literary question on 2 Kings 4:8 ff, *ibid*, pp 93 ff.

46. On the literary question, cf Schmitt, *Elisa*, pp 80-81.

47. The quotation from the *Aqhat Epic* is taken from G. R. Driver, *Canaanite Myths and Legends* (Edinburgh, 1956), p 55. On this epic, cf the summary in H. Gese, *Die Religionen Altsyriens*, Religionen der Menschheit (RM) 10.2 (Stuttgart, 1970), pp 87 ff. In the same work there is a detailed introduction to the Ugaritic religion.

48. The quotation from the Iliad is taken from the translation of Samuel Butler, ed. Louise Ropes Loomis, in the Classics Club ed. (New York, 1942), pp 323-24. On the acceptance of death on the part of Homeric characters, cf Fränkel, *Dichtung und Philosophie*, pp 89-90.

49. *Consolatio ad Apollonium* 119E.

50. Of course one must remember that in the Old Testament we have a highly one-sided selection from the literature of ancient Israel and must recall, e g, the lament over Saul and Jonathan in 2 Sam. 1:19 ff, in order to provide a healthy relativizing of the suggested contrast, at least with respect to the pre-exilic period.

51. Still, on this point cf M. Heidegger, *Being and Time*, John Macquarrie and Edward Robinson, trs. (London, 1962), § 50, pp 293 ff.

52. Cf below, pp 48-50. On the matter of solidarity, cf W. Schulz, "Zum Problem des Todes," in *Denken im Schatten des Nihilismus. Festschrift W. Weischedel* (Darmstadt, 1975), pp 313 ff.

53. *Apology* 29 A.

54. *Ibid*.

55. *Apology* 40 C.

56. Cf 40A with 41, and on this point cf W. K. C. Guthrie, *A History of Greek Philosophy* (Cambridge, 1969, 1975), Vol III, pp 402 ff.

57. *Apology* 41B. Cf also above p 18.

58. On this topic cf also A. de Saint-Exupéry, *Terre des Hommes*, Oeuvres, Bibliothèque de la Pléiade (Paris, 1953), pp 176 ff.

59. "Non fueram, non sum, nescio; non ad me pertinet," *Römische Grabinschriften*, H. Geist and G. Pfohl, eds., Tusculum-Bücherei (Munich, 2nd ed., 1976), p 164, n 433.

60. *Ibid*, n 434.

61. "Nil fui, nil sum; et tu, qui vivis, es bibe lude veni," *ibid*, pp 164-65, n 435.

62. *Apology* 40E-41C.

63. On the derivation of the word "Sheol," cf L. I. J. Stadelmann, *The Hebrew Conception of the World*, AnBib 39 (Rome, 1970), pp 165-66.

64. The series omitted belongs to an apocalypticizing revision that limits the sojourn in the underworld to the time prior to the resurrection.

65. It is God who is being addressed here.

66. On the translation of this passage, cf F. Stier, *Das Buch Ijob hebräisch und deutsch* (Munich, 1954), pp 70 ff, and H. Bobzin, *Die "Tempora" im Hiobdialog* (Dissertation, Marburg, 1974), pp 204 ff.

67. Cf e g, Ps. 8:13; 18:4 ff; 30:3; 71:20; 86:13; and 88:3 ff. On the discussion of the force of the conception, cf, e g, Chr. Barth, *Die Errettung vom Tode in den individuellen Klage und Dankliedern des Alten Testaments* (Zollikon, 1947), pp 80 ff, with L. Wächter, *Der Tod im Alten Testament* (Berlin/DDR and Stuttgart, 1964), pp 48 ff, and N. J. Tromp, *Primitive Conceptions of Death and the Nether World in the Old Testament*, Biblica et Orientalia (BibOr) 21 (Rome, 1969), pp 129 ff. On the idea of death as life in its very weakest form, cf A. R. Johnson, *The Vitality of the Individual in the Thought of Ancient Israel* (Cardiff, 2nd ed. 1964), p 88.

68. On this point, cf below, p 37.

69. Even though one may reasonably understand this only to be poetic adornment, still it points back to a corresponding popular belief.

70. In addition to these two, there is a third designation for the spirits of the dead; it was borrowed from the Akkadian *etimmu*, and originally referred to the spirits of the dead in general. Cf H. Wohlstein, "Zu den israelitischen Vorstellungen von Toten- und Ahnengeistern," *Biblische Zeitschrift*, N. F. 5 (1961), pp 35 ff; further F. Schmidtke, "Träume, Orakel und Totengeister als Künder der Zukunft in Israel und Babylonien," *Biblische Zeitschrift*, N. F. 11 (1967), pp 240 ff.

71. On this, see above, p 34.

72. Cf also J. Wellhausen, *Reste arabischen Heidentums* (Berlin, 2nd ed. 1897, 3rd ed. 1961), p 151. Gunkel's recollection (Genesis, *Handkommentar zum Alten Testament* I, 1, Göttingen, 3rd. ed., 1910, p 361) of Plautus, *Amphitryon* I. 3.34: "Cur me tenes? tempus est; exire ex urbe, priusquam lucescat volo" ("Why are you holding me? The time has come, and I mean to leave the city before dawn"), still deserves attention.

73. On this point cf R. Tischner, *Ergebnisse okkulter Forschung. Eine Einführung in die Parapsychologie* (Stuttgart, 1950), pp 167 ff.

74. On this point cf H. A. Hoffner, *Theologisches Wörterbuch zum Alten Testament* I, cols 141 ff.

75. Cf *Gilgamesh Epic*, Tablet XII.69 ff.

76. Cf also the *Iliad* XXIII.97 ff.

77. Cf W. F. Otto, *Die Manen oder von den Urformen des Totenglaubens* (Darmstadt, 2nd. ed., 1958, 3rd ed., 1976). To be sure Cicero, *Tusculan*

Disputations I.29, appears to me not to represent the dream-hypothesis so unequivocally and exclusively.

78. On this point cf Otto, pp 105 ff, who rightly recalls Justinus Kerner's "Seherin von Prevorst." That work has recently been reissued with a foreword by J. Bodamer (Stuttgart, 3rd ed., 1973). On this topic cf also A. Köberle, "Die Welt des Uebersinnlichen. Hindernis oder Hilfe auf dem Weg zum Glauben," *Neue Zeitschrift für Systematische Theologie* (NZSTH) 13 (1971), pp 176 ff, and the same author's "Das Weltbild der Parapsychologie. Wandlungen im Seelenverständnis der Gegenwart," in *Denkender Glaube. Festschrift C. H. Ratschow* (Berlin, 1976), pp 225 ff.

79. Cf, e g, the *Odyssey* X.495; XI.207; Sophocles, *Ajax* 1257; Euripides, fr. 532; further, Pindar, *Pythian Odes* 8.95. The Old Testament is familiar with the comparison of the fleeting, transitory life with a shadow (Ps. 102:11; cf Wisd. Sol. 2:5), but not the shadow as the soul of the deceased.

80. On this point cf below, pp 59-60.

81. Cf the verbal "nasham" in the reflexive N-stem in Isa. 42:14.

82. The meaning of "throat" is nicely documented in Isa. 5:14. The meaning of "breath" can only be postulated concerning the verbal N-stem with the connotation of "breathing deeply;" cf, e g, Exod. 23:12, and C. Westermann, *Theologisches Handwörterbuch zum Alten Testament* II, Col 73.

83. Cf F. Kluge, *Etymologisches Wörterbuch der deutschen Sprache*, ed. W. Mitzka with the assistance of A. Schirmer (Berlin, 17th ed. 1957), p 697.

84. Cf 2 Sam. 1:19 and the Ugaritic text in A. Herdner, *Corpus des tablettes en cunéiformes alphabétiques decouvertes à Ras Shamra - Ugarit de 1929–1939 (CTA)* 18:v.24-25.

85. For the resolution of the problem of continuity I assume the responsibility. On this matter, cf A. Schnaufer, *Frühgriechischer Totenglaube*, Spudasmata 20 (Hildesheim and New York, 1970), pp 58 ff and 198 ff. His study has eliminated the objections raised by Otto (pp 27 ff and 40 ff) to Rohde's views.

86. Cf Gen. 3:19, and on this same point, above, p 21.

87. On this point cf above, p 38.

88. On this point cf above, p 28.

89. On this point cf K. Seybold, *Das Gebet des Kranken im Alten Testament*, Beiträge zur Wissenschaft vom Alten und Neuen Testament (BWANT) 99 (Stuttgart, 1973), pp 123 ff.

90. On the Hebrew understanding of illness or other diminution of life as being delivered into the power of death, cf above, p 34, with n 67.

91. On this point cf above p 27.

92. On this point cf Milik (above, n 39), pp 25 and 28 ff, and esp p 31.

93. Cf 4QEn^b 1.III.11 (Milik, pp 171-72) and 4QEn^c 1.VI.1 (Milik, pp 192 and 194).

94. 4QEn^e 1.XXII margin 3-4 (Milik, p 229).

95. 4QEn^e 1.XXII margin 1, *Ibid.* In view of the Greek reading, *pneumata tōn psychōn tōn anthropōn* (cf M. Black, *Pseudepigrapha veteris testamenti Graecae* 3 [Leiden, 1970], ad loc) one can ask whether the original Aramaic text also spoke of the *ruchoth naphshoth kol bene 'anasha'*. With the fragmentary state of preservation of 4QEn^e 1.XXII, this would not be impossible.

96. On this point cf Rost (above, n 1), pp 123-24.

97. On this point cf above, pp 39-40.

98. Cf the translation in *APOT* II, pp 587 ff.

99. On the exegetical side, Bruce Vawter, "Intimations of Immortality and the Old Testament," *Journal of Biblical Literature (JBL)* 91 (1972), pp 158 ff, has taken a comparable position and consequently has evoked a refutation by H. C. Brichto, *Hebrew Union College Annual* (HUCA) 44 (1973), pp 1 ff.

100. Cf Isa. 14:9; 26:14, 19; Ps. 88:10; Prov. 2:18; 9:18; 21:16; and Job 26:5.

101. *Kanaanäische und aramäische Inschriften (KAI)* 13:8; 14:8; 117:1. In the last-named, bilingual Latin and Punic inscription, there is, as the Latin equivalent, "dis manibus," the "good gods" or "manes." On this point cf K. Latte, *Römische Religionsgeschichte*, Handbuch der Altertumswissenschaft (HAW) V.4 (Munich, 1960, 1967), pp 99-100.

102. On this point cf above, p 39. The Hebrew could have detected in the word *rephaim* either the verb *rafa'*, "to heal," or the verb *rafah*, "to grow weary or slack."

103. Cf *CTA* 20-22 and the translation in *ANET*, pp 149*b*-51*a*; and on this; A. Caquot, "Les rephaims ougaritiques," *Syria* 37 (1960), pp 74 ff; H. Gese, *Religionen*, p 91; further, Hesiod, *Works and Days* 109-26, and on this point, E. Rohde, *Psyche*, pp 253 ff.

104. Thus the Sumerian or Akkadian description of the underworld. Cf Friedr. Delitzsch, *Das Land ohne Heimkehr* (Stuttgart, 1911), pp 14 and 36-37, with n 21; but also K. Tallqvist, *Sumerisch-akkadische Namen der Totenwelt*, Studia Orientalia (StOr) v 4 (Helsinki and Leipzig, 1934), p 15.

105. On this point cf. above, p 33.

106. An earlier connection may be indicated by the Sumerian idea that the sun was visible by night to the deceased, and in the days of the dark of the moon, the moon as well. On this see S. N. Kramer, "Death and the Nether World according to the Sumerian Literary Texts," *Iraq* 22 (1960), p 63. On the Egyptian ideas, cf H. Kees, *Totenglaube und Jenseitsvorstellungen der alten Aegypter* (Berlin, 2nd. ed. 1956).

107. *CTA* 4:VII. 47-48; cf the translation by J. C. de Moor, *The Seasonal Pattern in the Ugaritic Myth of Baelu*, Alter Orient und Altes Testament (AOAT) 16 (Kevelaer and Neukirchen, 1971), p 164.

108. About this deity, cf Gese, *Religionen*, pp 135 ff.

109. On the names, cf G. Widengren, *Vetus Testamentum* 4 (1954), pp 98-99, and N. J. Tromp, *Primitive Conceptions*, pp 54 ff.

110. Cf *CTA* 4:VIII.9 ff; and the translation in *ANET*, p 135, as well as CTA 6:VI.28.

111. Cf *CTA* 4:VIII.1 ff with 5:V.11 ff, and on the meaning of *knkny*, J. C. de Moor, *JNES* 24 (1965), p 363, n 68, or the same author's *Seasonal Pattern*, pp 170-71. On this matter cf also H. Schmökel, *Das Gilgamesch Epos* (Stuttgart, 1966), p 81 (Tablet IX. II.1 ff, Assyrian Version).

112. *Odyssey* X.508 ff; Virgil, *Aeneid* VI.295 ff, and on this, E. Norden, *P. Vergilius Maro Aeneis Buch VI* (Darmstadt, 6th ed., 1976), p 220; and Plato,*Phaedo* 112E-113C, and on this, P. Friedländer, *Platon* I, pp 276 ff.

113. Schmökel, pp 89 ff (*Gilgamesh Epic*, Tablet X), and above, pp 25-26.

114. Cf the portrayal of Charon in Vergil, *Aeneid* VI.298 ff, and on this matter, V. von Geisau, *Kleine Pauly (KP)* 1, cols 1138-39.

115. On the pit, *shachat*, cf, e g, Job 33:18, 30; Jonah 2:7. On the cistern, *bor*, cf Ps. 88:4; Isa. 38:18.

116. Cf Ps. 88:11; Job 26:6; Prov. 15:11; 27:20 (both Sheol and Abaddon here); personified, Job 28:22 and Rev. 9:11. On the translation, cf Stadelman, p 168.

117. Cf M. Tsevat, *Vetus Testamentum* 4 (1954), pp 43 ff; H. Bobzin, *Die "Tempora" im Hiobdialog*, pp 420-21.

118. On this point cf E. Cassirer, *Philosophie der symbolischen Formen. II. Das Mythische Denken* (Darmstadt, 2nd ed., 1953), pp 93 ff, and H. Frankfort, *Ancient Egyptian Religion* (New York, 2nd ed., 1949) p 4.

119. Cf *CTA* 5:II.2 ff with 5:V.5 ff; tr. in *ANET*, pp 138-39.

120. *Tusculan Disputations* I.XVI.36.

121. Cf J. Wiesner, *Grab und Jenseits. Untersuchungen im ägäischen Raum zur Bronzezeit und frühen Eisenzeit*, Religionsgeschichtliche Versuche und Vorarbeiten 26 (Berlin, 1938), p 166.

122. On this point cf also Wiesner, pp 163 ff; further, J. Maringer, *Vorgeschichtliche Religion* (Einsiedeln-Zurich-Cologne, 1956), pp 76-77, 118-19, and esp. 121-22.

123. Wiesner, p 165. Cf also K. M. Kenyon, *Archaeology in the Holy Land* (London, 1960), pp 52 ff.

124. Wiesner, p 167.

125. Cf G. Hölscher, *Geschichte der israelitischen und jüdischen Religion* (Giessen, 1922), p 44.

126. Cf J. Mellaart, *The Neolithic in the Near East* (London, 1975), p 89 (Alikosh in the Zagros region); there is a similar find, dating from about 5000 B.C., in Siyalik I on the northern Iranian plateau; cf *ibid*, pp 187-88.

127. On this point cf Maringer, p 76, with illustration 3 on p 74.

128. On this point cf Wiesner, p 203.

129. Cf the finds presented in Mellaart, pp 37-38; p 35, fig 4; pp 61-62; p 79; p 82; p 89; pp 101 ff; p 131; pp 150-51; pp 187-88, p 191, p 207, p 221, (p 251), with those on p 111, p 137, p 146, pp 159-60, p 176, pp 178-79, p 193, p 216, p 225; p 235, p 238, and p 257.

130. On this point cf above, p 38.

131. Wiesner, p 168.

132. On this point cf below, pp 48-49.

133. Schmökel, p 120 (*Gilgamesh Epic*, Tablet XII.155 ff). Cf also E. Ebeling, *Tod und Leben nach den Vorstellungen der Babylonier, 1. Teil: Texte* (Berlin and Leipzig, 1931), p 147.

134. Thus Jeanne-Marie Aynard, "Le jugement des morts chez les Assyro-Babyloniens," in *Le jugement des morts*, Sources orientales 4 (Paris, 1961), p 84.

135. On this point, cf e g, J. Nahev, *Israel Exploration Journal* (IEJ) 13 (1963), p 90. On the omission of the offerings, which was exceptional, cf *ibid*, pp 89-90. In the course of time they became less common, and they are totally absent from the cemetery at Qumran; this is noted by R. de Vaux, *Les institutions de l'Ancien Testament* I (Paris, 1958), pp 98-99, and the same author's *Archaeology and the Dead Sea Scrolls* (London, 1973), pp 45 ff.

136. Contra F. Schwally, *Das Leben nach dem Tode nach den Vorstellungen des alten Israels und des Judentums einschliesslich des Volksglaubens im Zeitalter Christi* (Giessen, 1892), p 23, and Wächter (above, n 67), pp 185-86, and in agreement with Naveh, p 90, note 38, and H. C. Brichto, "Kin, Cult, and After-life—A Biblical Complex," *HUCA* 44 (1973), p 29, one should not regard Deut. 26:14 as an absolute prohibition of providing food for the dead. On this practice cf also Tob. 4:17, and see Wächter, p 183 ff.

137. If one observes in the Mycenaean burials on the one hand the inclusion of gold masks, and on the other hand the rough, rude treatment of offerings and skeletal remains from earlier burials when the same tombs are used for later

burials, it is doubtful whether the two phenomena are to be explained in terms of the belief in the "living corpse" and its diminishing strength, as A. Schnaufer (above, n 85) suggests, pp 8 ff. Even if it is preferable to explain the masks with the use of these conceptions, in view of the treatment of the dismembered skeletons it must be asked whether this treatment does not rather already presuppose the idea of the journey of the soul: after the soul of the departed has reached its goal, the careful treatment of the skeleton, which in the meantime has been dismembered, could be regarded as unnecessary. If it can be assumed that up until that time the deceased person had a rightful claim to respectful treatment, then one may infer (with Wiesner, pp 170-71) from the fact that the offerings along with the skeletons were pushed to the back of the tomb and thus were treated as "taboo," that the dismemberment of the skeleton was not regarded as an indication of the dissolution of the life of the dead hereafter. The finds from the Middle Bronze age summarized by K. M. Kenyon, pp 189 ff, could be interpreted in the sense of an overlapping of the ideas of the "living corpse" and the journey of the departed into the underworld. Finally, in this connection it may be remarked that the sacrifice of living persons (on this cf J. C. Gadd, "The Spirit of Living Sacrifices in Tombs," *Iraq* 22 [1960], pp 51 ff, and Schnaufer, pp 16-17) of course can also be connected with the intention to provide the needed servants for the journey into the realm of the dead and for the deceased person's appearance there in keeping with his status, as little as it can be connected with the shadowy realm of later times. Our attention has already been called, in connection with what the biblical material says about the rephaim, to the fact that the idea of the sojourn in the underworld must have changed in the course of the millennia.

138. In addition to Kees (above, n 106), cf also, e g, A. Erman, *Die Religion der Aegypter* (Berlin and Leipzig, 1934, 1968), pp 206 ff, and the graphic chapter, "Es spukt," in Emma Brunner-Traut, *Die Alten Aegypter. Verborgenes Leben Unter den Pharaonen* (Stuttgart, 1974), pp 174 ff.

139. Brunner-Traut, p 174.

140. On this, cf n 70, above.

141. Ebeling, p 147.

142. *Gilgamesh Epic*, Tablet XII.149 ff. Cf also p 31, above.

143. Cf the *Iliad* XXIII.65 ff, and the *Odyssey* XI.51 ff; and on this Rohde, *Psyche*, pp 18-19, as well as Schnaufer, *Totenglaube*, pp 71 ff, along with pp 46 ff, 58 ff, and 69-70.

144. *Aeneid* VI.297-332. The tr. is from *Vergil*, with an Eng. Tr. by H. Rushton Fairclough (London and New York, 1922), Vol. I, pp 527-29.

145. On the significance of ceremonies for the deceased as rituals of release, cf also P. Radin, "Gott und Mensch in der primitiven Welt," *The World of Primitive Man* (Zurich, n. d.) pp 169 ff.

146. A break in the overall picture first comes about through the poetic dissolution of the correspondence, otherwise realistically viewed, between the fate of a person in the tomb and one's fate in the underworld; this dissolution was accomplished in the book of Ezekiel, and it was resolved in favor of the latter. On this point, cf W. Zimmerli, *Ezechiel*, Biblischer Kommentar (BK) XIII.2 (Neukirchen, 1969), pp 785-86.

147. Cf Gen. 25:8, 35:29; further, Job 42:17; Gen. 49:29; and Deut. 32:50.

148. Thus also E. M. Myers, "Secondary Burial in Palestine," *Biblical Archaeology* (BA) 33 (1970), p 17.

149. Cf Gen. 25:8 with 25:9-10; 35:29 with 25:17; 49:29-31 with 50:13;

50:25-26 with Josh. 24:32; 2 Sam. 19:38, and on this verse see above, p 30; Neh. 2:3; further, Amos 7:17.

150. It may be noted that in view of the dependence upon sons to perform proper burial and to provide food for the dead, a special importance was attached to having sons as those who would perform these tasks. On this point, cf e g Schwally (above, n 136), p 28. On the corresponding obligation of the "redeemer," cf Brichto, *HUCA* 44, p 21.

151. Here presumably the beginnings of songs of lamentation are being quoted; cf W. Rudolph, *Jeremia*, Handbuch zum alten Testament (HAT) I, 12 (Tübingen, 3rd ed., 1968), p 142, on this passage.

152. *KAI* 14.7 ff. Ghost stories are not to be expected in the Old Testament, by the very nature of the literature; cf, however, Jer. 31:15, and further, 2 Macc. 15:11 ff. The later Jewish ideas are marked by the ideas of the Old Testament. Cf R. Meyer, *Hellenistisches in der rabbinischen Anthropologie*, BWANT 74 (Stuttgart, 1934), p 1 ff. On the refusal of burial as divine punishment cf also Jer. 7;33; 16:4. On the same refusal as human punishment, cf, e g, Sophocles, *Antigone* 998 ff; 1064 ff; Suetonius, *Life of Augustus* 13.

153. On this point cf also above, pp 53.

154. On this point cf R. de Vaux, *Institutions* I, pp 95 96.

155. On this point cf J. M. C. Toynbee, "Death and Burial in the Roman World," in *Aspects of Greek and Roman Life* (London, 1971), p 49. On the burial of slaves and criminals among the Greeks, cf D. C. Kurtz and J. Boardman, "Greek Burial Customs," in *Aspects of Greek and Roman Life*, pp 198-99. On the question of the immortality of slaves, however, cf also Plato, *Meno* 82A-85B.

156. On Ezek. 28:8 cf Zimmerli, BK XIII.2, p 669.

157. On the repeatedly expanded basic text cf Zimmerli, *op cit*, p 780. On the correspondence, even in what was included in the tomb at burial, cf 32:27.

158. Cf O. Eissfeldt, "Schwerterschlagene bei Hesekiel," in *Kleine Schriften* III (Tübingen, 1966), pp 6 ff.

159. Cf *KAI* 13; 14; 191; K. Galling, *Textbuch zur Geschichte Israels* (Tübingen, 2nd ed. 1968), Text 23 B; D. D. Luckenbill, *Ancient Records of Assyria and Babylonia* II (Chicago, 1927; New York, 1965), § 810, end.

160. Luckenbill, § 810, end.

161. Cf also the threat that the bodies would be eaten by wild birds and animals, in Deut. 28:26; Ezek. 29:4-5, 32:1 ff; and 39:17 ff, as well as 1 Sam. 17:44 ff.

162. Cf also Sophocles, *Antigone* 72 ff, 450 ff, and 1347 ff.

163. Cf further Horace, *Carmina* I.28.

164. *Rephaim*. On this topic, cf above, pp 41-42.

165. That is, an aborted fetus.

166. That is, those who have been executed.

167. On the entire poem, cf also O. Kaiser, *Der Prophet Jesaja. Kapitel 13-39*, ADT 18 (Göttingen, 2nd ed., 1976), pp 25 ff.

168. On this point cf also Joachim Jeremias, *New Testament Theology I: The Proclamation of Jesus* (New York, 1971), p 184.

169. On this matter, cf also n 1, above.

170. The special position held by the Egyptians' belief about the dead certainly is a consequence of the central position provided for the sun in their religion. The sun, which people saw traversing the heavens during the day, was thought of as being in a subterranean counter-heaven during the night.

171. On this point, cf Rose (above, n 23), p 49.

172. On this point, cf K. Reinhard, *Die Ilias und ihr Dichter*, U. Hölscher, ed. (Göttingen, 1961), p 383.

173. On this point, cf H. Gese (above, n 47), pp 51 ff; further, O. Kaiser, *Die mythische Bedeutung des Meeres in Aegypten, Ugarit und Israel*, BZAW 68 (Berlin, 2nd ed. 1962), pp 44 ff.

174. On this point, cf, e g, W. H. Schmidt, *Alttestamentlicher Glaube in seiner Geschichte* (Neukirchen, 2nd. ed., 1975).

175. Cf also G. Hölscher (above, n 125), p 46, n 17.

176. Cf also Deut. 32:39. On this phenomenon cf also above p 34.

177. The quotation is taken from *Homer; The Iliad*, with an Eng. tr. by A. T. Murray (Cambridge and London, 1957), Vol II, pp 469-71. On this passage, cf Reinhard (above, n 170), pp 382 ff.

178. Rephaim. Cf above, pp 41-42.

179. Cf, e g, Num. 5:2; Lev. 21:1 ff; Ezek. 44:25.

180. Euripides, *Hippolytus* 1437. Additional documentation is given by W. F. Otto, *Die Götter Griechenlands* (Frankfurt, 2nd ed., 1934; 6th ed., 1970), p 136.

181. On the basic meaning of Ps. 31:5, whose interpretation has been determined by Luke 23:46, cf K. Seybold (above, n 89), p 72.

182. In Egyptian religion, complicated ceremonies of purification were required for the deceased person before he was permitted to enter the realm of the gods. On this point, cf, e g, H. Bonnet, *Reallexikon der ägyptischen Religionsgeschichte* (Berlin and New York, 1952, 2nd ed., 1971), pp 635-36.

183. Cf E. Brunner, *The Christian Doctrine of Creation and Redemption* (Philadelphia, 1952), p 13; G. Fohrer, *Theologische Grundstrukturen des Alten Testaments* (Berlin and New York, 1972), pp 95 ff.

184. Cf Ps. 115:17-18, and on this subject cf also G. Schunack, *Das hermeneutische Problem des Todes im Horizont von Römer 5 untersucht*, Hermeneutische Unterschungen zur Theologie (HUTh) 7 (Tübingen, 1967), pp 63 ff.

185. Rephaim; cf above, pp 41-42.

186. Cf above, p 50.

187. *Odyssey* XI.487 ff; cf above, p 43.

188. The arms.

189. The back.

190. The teeth

191. The eyes.

192. The ears.

193. White hair.

194. The meaning of the metaphors employed here is disputed. Many think that this is an intentionally obscure use of symbolic words that have an erotic significance.

195. The poet here is thinking of a lamp hanging from the ceiling as a symbol of life; cf Job 18:5-6; 38:15.

196. On this point cf also O. Kaiser, "Der Mensch unter dem Schicksal," *NZSTh* 14 (1972), pp 22 ff.

197. Cf Jer. 20:14 ff; Job 3:2 ff; 10:18. The difference between the wish manifested in Ecclesiastes and the passages cited here lies in the difference in situation: in the former, we have the result of reflection, with a generalizing tendency, and in the latter, the expression of doubt and despair over one's own lot.

198. *Phaedo* 62C. On the divergent attitude of the Stoics, cf, e g, Seneca, *De*

providentia VI.7: "patet exitus: si pugnare non vultis, licit fugere" ("The way out is open; if you do not wish to fight, it is permissible to flee").

199. On this point cf Wächter, *Tod* (above,n 67), pp 89 ff; and on 2 Sam. 31:4-5, cf also H. J. Stoebe, *Das erste Buch Samuelis*, Kommentar zum Alten Testament (KAT) VIII.1 (Gütersloh, 1973), p 527: "Die Tat Sauls ist nur Anerkennung eines Schicksals, das bereits entschieden ist" ("Saul's act is only a recognition of a fate that is already decided").

200. Flavius Josephus, *War of the Jews* VII.389-401.

201. *Ibid*, VII.325.

202. Horace, in the last strophe of his ode that is famous for its opening words, "Nunc est bibendum, nunc pede libero pulsanda tellus," praises the dying Cleopatra as "deliberata morte ferocior," as "in voluntary death of even a loftier kind." Vergil, in the *Aeneid* VI.434 ff, assigns to suicides a special place in the underworld that is flooded nine times by the river Styx, and represents them as wishing in vain to be back in the poverty and drudgery of earthly life.

203. On the question of the Sitz-im-Leben of Ps. 39, cf Seybold (above, n 89), pp 129 ff.

204. On this point, cf V. Tzaferis, "Jewish Tombs at and near Giveat Ha-Mivtar," *IEJ* 20 (1970), pp 18 ff; N. Haas, "Anthropological Observations on the Skeletal Remains from Giveat Ha-Mivtar," *ibid*, pp 38 ff; further, M. Hengel, "Mors stupissima crucis. Die Kreuzigung in der antiken Welt und die 'Torheit' des 'Wortes vom Kreuz'," in *Rechtfertigung. Festschrift E. Käsemann* (Tübingen and Göttingen, 1976), pp 125 ff.

205. Cf Table III in N. Haas' article in *IEJ* 20, p 45.

206. On the Sitz-im-Leben of the psalm, cf Seybold (above, 89), pp 142 ff.

207. Cf, e g, Job 30:1 ff; Ps. 22:7-8; 69:11-12; and 1 Kings 17:18 as well. On an understanding, with affinities with the Old Testament, of illness and untimely, "bad" death, cf, e g, A. E. Jensen, *Mythos und Kult bei den Naturvölkern* (Wiesbaden, 2nd ed., 1960), pp 354 ff and 363 ff; on the subject of a "bad" death cf also H. J. Sell, *Der schlimme Tod bei den Völkern Indonesiens* (The Hague, 1955).

208. Cf, e g, Exod. 20:5; 34:7; 2 Sam. 12:15 ff; and the objection voiced in Job 21:19.

209. It should be noted that this formulation goes back to Kant; reference may be made, e g, to his Critique of Judgment.

210. On this point cf W. F. Albright, "Northwest Semitic Names in a List of Egyptian Slaves from the Eighteenth Century B.C.," *Journal of the American Oriental Society (JAOS)* 74 (1954), pp 223 ff, or G. Fohrer, *Das Buch Hiob*, KAT XVI (Gütersloh, 1963), pp 71-72.

211. On the literary problems, cf, e g, O. Kaiser, *Einleitung in das Alte Testament* (Gütersloh, 3rd ed., 1975), pp 347 ff; on the prologue, now cf also L. Schmidt, *De Deo*, BZAW 143 (Berlin and New York, 1976), pp 165 ff; on the theological stratification, cf, e g, O. Kaiser, "Leid und Gott," in *Sichtbare Kirche. Festschrift H. Laag* (Gütersloh, 1973), pp 13 ff.; on the religio-historical problem, cf H. Gese, *Lehre und Wirklichkeit in der alten Weisheit* (Tübingen, 1958); J. Gray, "The Book of Job in the Context of Near Eastern Literature," *Zeitschrift für die Alttestamentliche Wissenschaft* (ZAW) 82 (1970), pp 251 ff.

212. On this point, cf above, p 16-17.

213. On the historical connections, cf A. H. J. Gunneweg, *Geschichte Israels bis Bar Kochba*, Theologische Wissenschaft (ThW) 2 (Stuttgart, 2nd ed., 1976), pp 113 ff.

214. On literary criticism here cf J. Garscha, *Studien zum Ezechielbuch*, Europäische Hochschulschriften. Reihe 23: Theologie (EHS.T) XXIII.23 (Bern and Frankfurt, 1974), pp 21 ff, 305, and 311.

215. On the different positions, cf, e g, E. Würthwein, "Gott und Mensch in Dialog und Gottesreden des Buches Hiob," in *Wort und Existenz* (Göttingen, 1970), pp 226 ff.

216. The question whether 21:22 is a redactional addition or is an original part of the text deserves consideration.

217. On this point cf H. Jonas, *Organismus und Freiheit. Ansätze zu einer philosophischen Biologie* (Göttingen, 1973), pp 42 ff.

218. Cf Kaiser in *Sichtbare Kirche* (above, n 211), pp 15-16.

219. On this point, cf above, pp 32 and 61-62.

220. Cf the documented discussion in W. Tarn and G. T. Griffith, *Hellenistic Civilization* (London, 3rd ed., 1952) p 254.

221. On Eccles. 4:1-3, cf above, p 63.

222. The Hebrew word here in each case is *hokhmah*.

223. On this point, cf K. Galling, "Der Prediger," in *Die fünf Megillot*, Handbuch zum Alten Testament (HAT) I.18 (Tübingen, 2nd. ed. 1969), pp 96-97.

224. On this question, cf Rost (aove, n 1), pp 64 ff.

225. On this point, cf also O. Kaiser, "Die Begründung der Sittlichkeit im Buche Jesus Sirach," *Zeitschrift für Theologie und Kirche (ZThK)* 58 (1958), pp 51 ff.

226. Following the translation of V. Ryssel in *APAT* I, pp 293-94. On the text, cf now also Fr. Vattoni, *Ecclesiastico*, Pub. Sem. Semit. Testi I (Naples, 1968), pp 58-59, and H. P. Rüger, *Text und Textform im hebräischen Sirach*, BZAW 112 (Berlin, 1970), p 17.

227. On this point cf Th. Middendorp, *Die Stellung Jesu Ben Siras zwischen Judentum und Hellenismus* (Leiden, 1973), p 17: on the cultural encounter of Judaism and Christianity, cf also M. Hengel, *Judaism and Hellenism: Studies in Their Encounter in Palestine during the Early Hellenistic Period*, John Bowden, tr. (Philadelphia, 1974), 2 vols.

228. Cf Eccles. 12:9.

229. On this point, cf above, pp 21 and 40.

230. Cf above, p 32.

231. On this point, cf e g, Job 17:16; Ps. 119:25; further, Tromp (above, n 67), pp 83 ff, who rightly recalls the portrayal of the underworld in the Babylonian "Descent of Ishtar into Hades," line 11, where it is said that there "dust is strewn on the door and the latch" (*AOT*, p 206; *ANET*, p 107).

232. The position of 12:5b in the context appears to me not to be entirely certain, though it fits in with the perspective of the preacher. (Translator's note: on the basis of this judgment, the author omitted this part of the verse in his quotation of Eccles. 11:9–12:6, above, pp 61-62. We have included it, however as part of the RSV which we have used). On the literary relationships of the little book, cf F. Ellermeier, *Qohelet* I.1 (Herzberg/Harz, 1967), and K. Galling, *HAT* I.18; with the latter, I regard 12:7 as redactional.

233. "Haec domus aeterna est, hic sum situs, hic ero semper," *Römische Grabinschriften* (above, n 59), p 166, No 441.

234. Cicero, *Tusculan Disputations* I.X.21.

235. "Adeone me delirare censes, ut ista esse credam?" ("Do you think I am out of my mind, that I should believe there is any such?"), *Tusculan Disputations* I.V.10.

236. Cf his *Necymantia* or his *De luctu*.

237. It is to be inferred from 5:1 ff.

238. On the problem of faith, cf above, pp 14-15; on this historical background of the religious persecutions of the second century B.C., cf E. Bickermann, *Der Gott der Makkabäer* (Berlin, 1937); Hengel (above, n 227), pp 283 ff; and more briefly, Gunneweg (above, n 212), pp 151 ff.

239. On the Sadducees and Pharisees, cf, e g, J. Wellhausen, *Die Pharisäer und die Sadduzäer* (Greifswald, 1874; Göttingen, 3rd ed. 1967); or, in very brief form, Gunneweg, p 165.

240. On this point, cf, e g, F. Nötscher, *Altorientalischer und alttestamentlicher Auferstehungsglaube* (1926), J. Scharbert, ed. (Darmstadt, 1970), pp 147-48; more recently, and in detail, W. Zimmerli, BK XIII.2, pp 885 ff, and in more concise form, the same author's *Ezechiel. Gestalt und Botschaft*, Biblische Studien (BSt) 62 (Neukirchen, 1972), pp 109 ff. On literary criticism and dating, cf also Garscha (above, n 214), pp 219 ff, 302, and 310-11. If one follows G. Jahn, *Das Buch Ezechiel auf Grund der Septuaginta hergestellt* (Leipzig, 1905), p 255 (in Garscha, p 222), and detaches 37:13b-14 as an addition, still it is necessary, in my opinion, seriously to consider whether the person who provided this addition, who is hardly to be placed before the end of the fourth century B.C., did not already understand the vision of the valley of dry bones as a prediction of the resurrection.

241. Cf also Martin-Achard (above, n 19), p 85. On this matter cf also K. Schubert, "Die Entwicklung der Auferstehungslehre von der nachexilischen bis zur frührabbinischen Zeit," *Biblische Zeitschrift* (BZ) N. F. 6 (1962), pp 177 ff.

242. Sanhedrin XI.1. Cf also the Gemara, fol. 90b to 91a. By the Mishna in this connection we mean the collection of rabbinical teachings that was compiled in the second century A.D. by Rabbi Judah the Prince. The Gemara contains the teachings of the Amoraim ("spokesmen"), from the closing of the Mishna down to the fifth century. By the Talmud we mean the combination of the Mishna and the Gemara. The word signifies study as well as instruction, especially concerning obedience to the Law. On this matter, cf H. L. Strack, *Einleitung in den Talmud* (Leipzig, 1908); Ch. Albeck, *Einführung in die Mischna* (Berlin, 1971).

243. Cf, e g, J. Buitkamp, *Die Auferstehungsvorstellungen in den Qumrantexten* (Dissertation, Groningen, 1964), p 20; E. Haenchen, "Auferstehung im Alten Testament," in *Die Bibel und wir. Gesammelte Aufsätze* II (Tübingen, 1968), p 88; G. Fohrer, *History of Israelite Religion*, David E. Green, tr. (Nashville, 1972), p 389. Wächter (above, n 67), p 194, admits Isa. 26:19 along with Daniel 12.

244. On this point, cf above, p 41.

245. Thus also, or somewhat similarly, e g, C. A. Briggs, *The Book of Psalms* I, International Critical Commentary (ICC) (Edinburgh, 1906), p 411; R. Kittel, *Die Psalmen*, KAT XIII (Leipzig, 5th and 6th eds., 1929), pp 367-68; G. von Rad, *Old Testament Theology* (New York, 1967), Vol I, p 406; H. J. Kraus, *Psalmen I*, BK XV.1 (Neukirchen, 1960), pp 367-68; M. Dahood, *Psalms I*, Anchor Bible 16 (Garden City, N.Y., 1965), p 301; in cautious agreement, Fohrer (above, n 243), p 386; with reservations, A. Weiser, *Die Psalmen*, ATD 14/15 (Göttingen, 5th ed., 1959), p 263; contra, Chr. Barth (above, n 67), pp 158 ff; Buitkamp (above, n 243), p 13.

246. The alignment of opinions pretty much corresponds to that with reference to Ps. 49, as noted above. This time Weiser opts for the interpretation that what is meant is the elimination of the boundaries and limitations of death (p 350). Fohrer (p 389) thinks it has reference to a deliverance in this life. E.

Würthwein, "Erwägungen zu Psalm 73" (above, n 215), pp 170-71, regards the psalm as a royal prayer and, referring to Isa. 36:17, understands the *laqach* to have an immanent import.

247. On this point cf also H. Gese, *Psalm 22 und das Neue Testament*, Beiträge zur evangelischen Theologie (BEvTh) 64 (Munich, 1974), pp 180 ff.

248. Cf Milik (above, n 39), pp 4 ff.

249. Under the influence of God's "dew of light" the earth is to bring forth the shades, the *rephaim* (cf above, p 42). The realistic feature is brought in with the insertion, "Thy dead shall live, my body shall rise." Cf also Kaiser, ATD 18, 2nd ed., pp 173 ff, on this passage.

250. On the age of 2 Macc. 7, cf Chr. Habicht, *Jüdische Schriften aus hellenistischer-römischer Zeit (JSHRZ)* I.3 (Gütersloh, 1976), pp 171-176. One may compare this in substance also with Syriac Baruch 50-51 (*APAT* II, p 430).

251. On this point, cf also Jeremias (above, n 167), p 180, n 28, and pp 237-38.

252. On this point, cf E. Lohse, below, pp. 138 ff.

253. Genesis 10-11; that is, since the Deluge.

254. On the seven archangels, cf Enoch 20:1 ff, and on this point, H. Bietenhard, *Die Himmlische Welt im Urchristentum und Spätjudentum*, Wissenschaftliche Untersuchungen zum Neuen Testament (WUNT) 2 (Tübingen, 1951), pp 101 ff.

255. Cf, e g, Exod. 32:32; Jer. 22:30; and on this idea, Bietenhard (above, n 254), pp 231 ff.

256. Cf O. Plöger, *Das Buch Daniel*, KAT XVIII (Gütersloh, 1965), pp 165 and 171-72.

257. On this, cf above, p 77, with n 231.

258. This interpretation is not shared by, e g, H. H. Rowley, *The Relevance of Apocalyptic* (London, 2nd ed., 1947), pp 51-53; D. S. Russell, *The Method and Message of Jewish Apocalyptic* (London, 1964), pp 368-69; Hengel (above, n 227), p 196; G. W. E. Nickelsburg, *Resurrection, Immortality and Eternal Life in Intertestamental Judaism*, Harvard Theological Studies (HThS) 26 (Cambridge, 1972), p 23.

259. On the various possibilities for interpretation of Enoch 22, cf Nickelsburg (above, n 258), pp 136-37. T. F. Glasson, *Greek Influence in Jewish Eschatology* (London, 1961), pp 17-18, expresses himself in favor of the view of a presupposed resurrection of all the righteous.

260. On the Neo-Platonic conception, which belongs to an altogether different context, of the threefold death—first of the body, then of the soul, and then of the spirit—cf Plutarch, *De facie in orbe lunae* (On the face in the moon) 945*a-c*.

261. On this point, cf below, pp 90.

262. Cf Rost (above, n 1), pp 129 ff; Milik (above, n 39) p 58. Nickelsburg (above, n 259), pp 46-47, argues that Jub. 23:16-31 appeared before Daniel 11-12.

263. But cf also Schubert (above n 241), pp 193 ff.

264. Cf Milik (above, n 39), pp 47 ff.

265. Cf also Glasson (above, n 259), pp 17-18.

266. Cf also Kaiser, ATD 18, p 162.

267. There is a translation in *New Testament Apocrypha*, E. Hennecke, W. Schneemelcher, and R. McL. Wilson, eds., I (Philadelphia, 1963), p 475.

268. On this point, cf above, pp 12-14.

269. On this point, cf R. N. Frye, "Iran and Israel," in *Festschrift Eilers* (Wiesbaden, 1967), pp 74 ff.

270. Cf the concise survey in C. Colpe, *Die religionsgeschichtliche Schule und die Kritik ihres Bildes vom gnostischen Erlösermythus*, Forschungen zur Religion und Literatur des Neuen Testaments (FRLANT) 78 (Göttingen, 1961), pp 117 ff, or in G. Widengren, *Die Religionen Irans*, RM 14 (Stuttgart, 1965), pp 3 ff.

271. Cf the critical discussion of the history of research in this area in J. Duchesne-Guillemin, *The Western Response to Zoroaster* (Oxford, 1958).

272. On this point, cf, e g, W. Lentz, "Plutarch und der Zerwanismus," in *Yad-Name-ye Irani-ye Minorsky* (Teheran, 1969), pp 1 ff. I am deeply indebted to my colleague Lentz for the detailed conversations with him about the intricacies and the possibilities of his field of specialization. Where I have not taken seriously enough his proper warnings, I alone bear the responsibility.

273. On this point, cf K. Judeich, *Kleinasiatische Studien* (Marburg, 1892).

274. On this point, cf O. Kaiser, "Der geknickte Rohrstab," in *Wort und Geschichte. Festschrift K. Elliger*, AOAT 18 (Kevelaer and Neukirchen, 1973), pp 99 ff, and *ibid*, "Zwischen den Fronten," in *Wort, Lied, Gottesspruch. Festschrift J. Ziegler*, Forschung zur Bibel (FzB) 2 (Würzburg, 1972), pp 197 ff.

275. On this point cf Hengel (above, n 227), pp 277 ff.

276. On this point, cf e g, Franz König, *Zarathustras Jenseitsvorstellungen und das Alte Testament* (Vienna/Freiburg/Basel, 1964), p 125.

277. On this point, cf König (above, n 26), pp 4 ff; Widengren (above, n 270), pp 102 ff. On the judgment of the dead, cf also M. Mole, "Le jugement des morts dans l'Iran Préislamique," in *Le jugement des morts* (above, n 134), pp 143 ff. The texts in question are found in translation there.

278. Plutarch, *De Iside et Osiride* 370c; Felix Jacoby, *Die Fragmente der Griechischen Historiker* B 115, F 65; on this point cf also König (above, n 176), pp 128 ff.

279. On this point cf also O. Kaiser, "Das Geheimnis von Eleusis," *Die Karawane* 17 (1976), 3/4, pp 43 ff. Additional literature is cited there.

280. On this point, cf M. P. Nilsson, "Die astrale Unsterblichkeit und die kosmische Mystik," in *Opuscula selecta* III (1960), pp 250 ff. I am indebted to my colleague K. Abel for making this essay available to me.

281. Cf W. K. C. Guthrie, *Orpheus and Greek Religion. A study of the Orphic Movement* (London, 1935, 2nd ed., 1952) pp 156 ff; further, A. Dieterich, *Nekyia* (Leipzig and Berlin, 2nd ed., 1913 = Darmstadt, 3rd ed., 1969), pp 72 ff and 84 ff.

282. On this point cf E. Rohde (above, n 36), pp 467 ff; Dieterich (above, n 281), pp 113 ff; C. Hopf, *Antiken Seelenwanderungsvorstellungen* (Dissertation, Leipzig; Borna and Leipzig, 1934); H. W. Thomas, *Epekeina. Untersuchungen über das Ueberlieferungsgut in den Jenseitsmythen Platons* (Dissertation, Munich; Würzburg, 1938); Guthrie (above, n 281), pp 238 ff.

283. *Timaeus* 42B.

284. *Phaedo* 113D-114E.

285. On this point, cf F. Cumont, *After-Life in Roman Paganism* (New Haven, 1922), pp 91 ff, and now more recently W. Burkert, *Weisheit und Wissenschaft. Studien zu Pythagoras, Philolaos und Platon*, Erlanger Forschungen (ErF) 10 (Nürnberg, 1962), pp 335 ff.

286. However, cf 4 Esdras 7:78 ff.

287. *Politeia* 364B.

288. On this problem cf N. Scholl, *Tod und Leben* (Munich, 1974).

289. Cf A. Strobel, "Der Tod Jesu und das Sterben des Menschen nach Lukas 23,39-49," in *Der Tod—ungelöstes Rätsel oder überwundener Feind,* A Strobel, ed. (Stuttgart, 1974), pp 81-99, especially p 85.

290. *The Oxyrhynchus Papyri* I, No 115; cf A. Deissmann, *Light from the Ancient East,* Lionel R. M. Strachan, tr. (New York, 1927), p 176.

291. On this entire cluster of problems, cf J. Choron, *Der Tod im abendländischen Denken* (Stuttgart, 1967).

292. On Jewish apocalypticism, cf H. H. Rowley (above, n 258); J. Schreiner, *Alttestamentlich-Jüdische Apokalyptik* (Munich, 1969); *ibid,* "Die apokalyptische Bewegung," in J. Maier and J. Schreiner, *Literatur und Religion des Frühjudentums* (Würzburg/Gütersloh, 1973), p 214-53; W. Schmithals, *The Apocalyptic Movement,* John E. Steely, tr. (Nashville, 1975); E. Lohse, *The New Testament Environment,* John E. Steely, tr. (Nashville, 1976), pp 55-73.

293. A detailed analysis of these apocalyptic utterances is found in W. Harnisch, *Verhängnis und Verheissung der Geschichte. Untersuchungen zum Zeit- und Geschichtsverständnis im 4. Buch Esra und in der Syr. Baruchapokalypse* (Göttingen, 1969).

294. Thus Rabbi Ammi, about A.D. 300, Babylonian Talmud, Sabbath 55a.

295. On the explanation of Rom. 5:12-21, cf the commentaries, particularly E. Käsemann, *An die Römer* (Tübingen, 3rd ed., 1974), and the literature cited there.

296. Cf K. Rahner, *On the Theology of Death* (New York, 1961), p 57.

297. On the much-discussed problem of the Adam-Christ typology, cf E. Brandenburger, *Adam und Christus* (Neukirchen, 1962), and now most recently Käsemann (above, n 295), pp 131-50, and the literature mentioned there.

298. Cf G. Schunack, *Das hermeneutische Problem des Todes. Im Horizont von Römer 5 untersucht* (Tübingen, 1967), p 274.

299. Cf Käsemann (above, n 295), pp 147-48.

300. Cf E. Jüngel, *Death: The Riddle and the Mystery* (Philadelphia, 1975), pp 96-97.

301. On the delineation and exposition of the pre-Pauline tradition, cf the commentaries, particularly H. Conzelmann, *1 Corinthians: A Commentary on the First Epistle to the Corinthians,* James W. Leitch, tr. (Philadelphia, 1975), and the literature cited there, especially J. Jeremias, *The Eucharistic Words of Jesus,* Norman Perrin, tr. (New York, 1966), pp 101-5.

302. Cf Conzelmann (above, n 301), p 254, and the exegetes named there. On the problem as a whole, cf the thoroughgoing study by K. Lehmann, *Auferweckt am dritten Tag nach der Schrift* (Freiburg, 2nd ed., 1969).

303. On the analysis of the passion narrative, cf E. Lohse, *Die Geschichte des Leidens und Sterbens Jesu Christi* (Gütersloh, 2nd ed., 1967); G. Schneider, *Verleugnung, Verspottung und Verhör Jesu nach Lukas 22,54-71. Studien zur lukanischen Darstellung der Passion Jesu* (Munich, 1969); *ibid, Die Passion Jesu nach den drei älteren Evangelien* (Munich, 1973); E. Linnemann, *Studien zur Passionsgeschichte* (Göttingen, 1970); L. Schenke, *Studien zur Passionsgeschichte des Markus. Tradition und Reaktion in Markus 14, 1-42* (Würzburg/ Stuttgart, 1971).

304. Cf E. Dinkler, *Signum Crucis* (Tübingen, 1967), pp 150-53 and illustration 33a.

305. Cf H. Conzelmann, E. Flesseman-van Leer, E. Haenchen, E. Käsemann, E. Lohse, *Zur Bedeutung des Todes Jesu* (Gütersloh, 2nd ed.,

1967); E. Bizer, W. Fürst, J. F. G. Goeters, W. Kreck, W. Schrage, *Das Kreuz Jesu Christi als Grund des Heils* (Gütersloh, 1967); G. Delling, *Der Kreuzestod Jesu in der urchristlichen Verkündigung* (Berlin/Göttingen, 1972); further, *Zum Verständnis des Todes Jesu.* Stellungnahme des Theologischen Ausschusses und Beschluss der Synode der Evangelischen Kirche der Union (Gütersloh, 1968); F. Viering, *Der Kreuzestod Jesu. Interpretation eines theologischen Gutachtens* (Gütersloh, 2nd ed., 1970).

306. Cf W. Pannenberg, "Tod und Auferstehung in der Sicht christlicher Dogmatik," *Kerygma und Dogma* (KuD) 20 (1974), p 178.

307. Cf W. Thüsing, *Die Erhöhung und Verherrlichung Jesu im Johannesevangelium* (Münster, 2nd ed., 1970).

308. From the abundance of scholarly studies the following may be mentioned: K. H. Rengstorf, *Die Auferstehung Jesu* (Witten, 5th ed., 1960); E. Lohse, *Die Auferstehung Jesu Christi im Zeugnis des Lukasevangeliums* (Neukirchen, 1961); W. Marxsen, U. Wilckens, G. Delling, H. G. Geyer, *Die Bedeutung der Auferstehungsbotschaft für den Glauben an Jesus Christus* (Gütersloh, 7th ed., 1968); W. Marxsen, *The Resurrection of Jesus of Nazareth*, Margaret Kohl, tr. (Philadelphia, 1970); H. Grass, *Ostergeschehen und Osterberichte* (Göttingen, 4th ed., 1970); U. Wilckens, *Resurrection*, A. M. Stewart, tr. (Atlanta, 1978); additional literature is cited there.

309. Cf J. Schniewind, "Answer to Rudolf Bultmann," in *Kerygma and Myth: A Theological Debate*, H. W. Bartsch, ed., Reginald H. Fuller, tr. (London, 1953, 1962), p. 69.

310. Cf E. Güttgemanns, *Der leidende Apostel und sein Herr (Göttingen, 1966), p 92, n 109.*

311. On the exposition of 1 Cor. 15:6b, cf especially H. W. Bartsch, "Die Argumentation des Paulus in 1 Cor. 15,3-11," *Zeitschrift für die neutestamentliche Wissenschaft* (ZNW) 55 (1964), pp 261-74.

312. Cf P. v. d. Osten-Sacken, "Die Apologie des paulinischen Apostolats in 1 Kor. 15,1-11," ZNW 64 (1973), pp 245-62.

313. On the more detailed analysis of the Easter narratives, cf U. Wilckens, *Resurrection*, pp 27-73.

314. From the relevant literature the following may be noted: W. Nauck, "Die Bedeutung des leeren Grabes für den Glauben an den Auferstandenen," ZNW 47 (1956), pp 243-67; L. Schenke, *Auferstehungsverkündigung und leeres Grab* (Stuttgart, 1968); H. v. Campenhausen, *Der Ablauf der Osterereignisse und das leere Grab* (Heidelberg, 4th. ed., 1973); further suggestions are given there.

315. Cf O. Cullmann, *Immortality of the Soul; or Resurrection of the Dead? The Witness of the New Testament* (New York, 1958).

316. On the representation of the Jewish hope of resurrection, cf further U. Wilckens, *Resurrection*, pp 85-100.

317. For the explanation of this passage, in addition to the commentaries one should refer also to the following: J. Jeremias, *Unknown Sayings of Jesus*, Reginald H. Fuller, tr. (London, 1958), pp 64 ff; W. Harnisch, *Eschatologische Existenz. Ein exegetischer Beitrag zum Sachanliegen von 1. Thess. 4,13 bis 5,11* (Göttingen, 1973), as well as J. Becker, *Auferstehung der Toten im Urchristentum* (Stuttgart, 1976), pp 46-54.

318. Cf E. Lohse, "Apokalyptik und Christologie," in *Die Einheit des Neuen Testaments* (Göttingen, 1973), p 137.

319. Cf J. Schniewind, "Die Leugner der Auferstehung in Korinth," in *Nachgelassene Reden und Aufsätze* (Berlin, 1952), pp 110-39, as well as the

explanation of 1 Cor. 15, especially in Conzelmann (above, n 301), and the literature cited there.

320. Cf E. Jüngel (above, n 300), p 39.

321. On the peculiar practice of baptism for the dead, cf the commentaries on this passage, and M. Rissi, *Die Taufe für die Toten* (1962), and esp E. Dinkler, "Totentaufe," in *Die Religion in Geschichte und Gegenwart*, 3rd ed., VI. Col 958.

322. Cf J. Moltmann, *Theology of Hope* (New York, 1967), p 180.

323. Cf K. Barth, *The Resurrection of the Dead*, H. J. Stenning, tr. (New York, 1933), p 169; R. Bultmann, *Faith and Understanding* (New York, 1969), p 84.

324. In verse 46 we have a parenthetical comment that interrupts the connection and appends an explanation to verse 44*b*. First the earthly (or psychical) was created, and only then the spiritual. Thus the spirit is a gift of the end-time and does not stand, as the enthusiasts thought, at the very beginning of all history, so that in the "spiritual" man as it were the previously concealed distinctiveness of man was liberated. On the details cf the commentaries.

325. Cf Schniewind (above, n 319), p 139.

326. Cf R. Bultmann, *Faith and Understanding* I, p 67.

327. On the more specific justification for the assumption of an editorial revision, cf the commentaries on the gospel of John, and especially R. Bultmann, *The Gospel of John: A Commentary* (Philadelphia, 1971), and R. Schnackenburg, *Das Johannesevangelium* (Freiburg, 1971) on this passage, as well as Becker (above, n 317), pp 144-45.

328. On this problem, cf Bultmann (above, n 327), p 225, n 3, and particularly E. Schweizer, *Ego Eimi* (Göttingen, 2nd ed., 1965).

329. Cf Schweizer (above, n 328), p 165.

330. Martin Luther, Weimar Ed. 49, p 53.

331. Cf Jüngel (above, n 300), p 127.

332. Luther, Weimar Ed. 11, p 141.

333. Proserpina was the daughter of Zeus and of Demeter, the consort of Pluto, who had seized her and taken her away from her mother. In response to the urgent plea of her mother, Zeus decreed that Proserpina might return to the upper world for a part of the year, but would spend the other part of the year in the underworld with Pluto. Thus the threshold of Proserpina leads into the underworld.

334. Apuleius, *Metamorphoses* XI.23.

335. On the explanation, cf G. Bornkamm, "Taufe und neues Leben," in *Das Ende des Gesetzes, Paulusstudien* (Munich, 5th ed., 1966), pp 34-50.

336. On the explanation, cf the commentaries, esp. E. Lohse, *Die Briefe an die Kolosser und an Philemon* (Göttingen, 1968), on this passage.

337. Luther, Weimar Ed. 40, I, p 283.

338. Cf G. Schunack, *Das hermeneutische Problem des Todes* (Tübingen, 1967), p 233.

339. Luther, Weimar Ed. 54, p 491.